MW01231299

# The Process of Writing

## Composing Through Critical Thinking

*Roberta Allen, Ed.D.*
Western Michigan University

*Marcia Mascolini, Ph.D.*
Western Michigan University

Prentice Hall
Upper Saddle River, New Jersey 07458

**Library of Congress Cataloging-in-Publication Data**
Allen, Roberta [date]
The process of writing : composing through critical thinking / Roberta Allen, Marcia Mascolini.
p. cm.
Includes index.
ISBN 0-13-182114-8 (alk. paper)
1. English language—Rhetoric. 2. Critical thinking. 3. Business writing. I. Mascolini, Marcia V. II. Title.
PE1479.B87A45 1997
808′.042—dc20 96-522
CIP

*Director of Production and Manufacturing:* Bruce Johnson
*Managing Editor:* Mary Carnis
*Acquisitions Editor:* Elizabeth Sugg
*Editorial Assistant:* Kadijah Bell
*Cover Design:* Jayne Conte
*Manufacturing Buyer:* Edward O'Dougherty
*Editorial/production supervision and interior design:* Inkwell Publishing Services


A Simon & Schuster Company
Upper Saddle River, New Jersey 07458



Printed in the United States of America
10 9 8 7 6 5 4 3 2 1

ISBN 0-13-182114-8

PRENTICE-HALL INTERNATIONAL (UK) LIMITED, *London*
PRENTICE-HALL OF AUSTRALIA PTY. LIMITED, *Sydney*
PRENTICE-HALL OF CANADA INC., *Toronto*
PRENTICE-HALL HISPANOAMERICANA, S.A., *Mexico*
PRENTICE-HALL OF INDIA PRIVATE LIMITED, *New Delhi*
PRENTICE-HALL OF JAPAN, INC., *Tokyo*
PRENTICE-HALL OF SOUTHEAST ASIA PTE. LTD., *Singapore*
EDITORA PRENTICE-HALL DO BRASIL, LTDA., *Rio de Janeiro*

# Contents

**Preface** *vii*

**PART I**
**CRITICAL THINKING AND WRITING**

**1 Think Before You Write** *1*

Audience Analysis *2*
Purpose and Form *5*
Summary *6*
Exercises *7*

**2 Generate and Organize Information** *15*

Techniques for Generating Ideas *15*
Outlining *20*
Summary *24*
Exercises *26*

**3 Compose Paragraphs for Specific Purposes** *33*

Focused Topic Sentences *34*
Unify Supporting Sentences *37*
Coherence *37*
Putting Writing into Perspective *39*
Cases *40*
Summary *41*
Case Analysis and Response Checklist *42*
Paragraph Score Sheet *43*
Exercises *44*
Business Cases *47*
Science and Technology Cases *52*
Social Sciences and Liberal Arts Cases *57*

**PART II**
**BASIC WRITING FORMS**

**4 Description** *63*

Principles of Description *64*
Outline for a Description *65*
Spatial Relationships *67*
Summary *68*
Description Score Sheet *69*
Exercises *70*

**5 The Longer Message** *83*

Structure of the Longer Message *83*
Aids to the Reader *86*
Sample Report with Headings *90*
Summary *92*
Longer Message Score Sheet *93*
Exercises *94*
Cases *101*

**6 Process Description** *109*

Writing the Process Description *110*
Illustrating a Process Description *112*
Writing a Lab Report *113*

Format for a Formal Process Description *116*
Summary *118*
Process Description Score Sheet *119*
Exercises *120*
Cases *124*

**7 Compare and Contrast** *131*

Thinking Process *133*
Two Methods of Development *134*
Patterns of Organization for Comparison/Contrast *136*
Summary *137*
Comparison/Contrast Score Sheet *138*
Exercises *140*
Cases *143*

**8 Write Persuasively** *147*

Audience Analysis *148*
Developing a Key Argument *149*
Organizing Support *150*
Summary *152*
Persuasion Score Sheet *154*
Exercises *156*
Cases *161*

**APPENDIXES**

**A Letter and Memo Formats** *167*

**B Proposals and Progress Reports** *173*

**C Documenting Secondary Sources** *177*

**Index** *183*

# Preface

Writing and thinking skills develop together. Research confirms our experience that you will learn to write well by analyzing the purpose of your writing, evaluating your audience, and applying logic to message development. Critical thinking skills you will develop in the context of writing to specific audiences include the following:

- *Analysis:* Learning to see parts of a whole.
- *Synthesis:* Arranging parts to form the whole.
- *Evaluation:* Judging the value of diverse information.
- *Problem solving:* Defining a specific problem, developing criteria to evaluate a solution, and analyzing data using the criteria.

Assignments encourage you to use logic in writing paragraphs devoted to cases in specific subject areas. These are a few of the writing and thinking skills you will develop:

- Classification for outlining, process description, and comparison/contrast paragraphs.
- Description and definition useful in preparing informative reports, abstracts, and summaries.

- Inferential skills, such as interpreting information for uninformed audiences.
- Decision making skills required for analytical messages, such as factoring problems for subtopics in a report.

This text is designed to introduce you to writing and critical thinking skills together, using paragraph development as a mode for expression. The classification skills discussed in Chapters 1 and 2 provide a foundation for more complex writing and thinking skills called for in Chapters 3 through 8.

All assignments have been used successfully in the authors' classrooms, particularly as in-class exercises. Our goal is to provide concise writing instruction based on critical thinking skills most useful in a variety of disciplines. The exercises reflect an increasing, but not overwhelming, challenge as you progress through the material.

Not all assignments will require your instructors' evaluation and may be edited in peer groups before writing final drafts. Talking about your daily writing activities in small groups is often an effective way of thinking about purpose and audience for a piece of writing. Allow yourself time to revise and edit the writing after group or class discussions, your instructor's evaluation, or your own proofreading. With daily writing practice, constructive criticism, reinforced critical thinking patterns, and a reason to write, you will gain proficiency and confidence as a writer.

**Acknowledgments**

We would like to thank our students for their insight into writing and their recognition of the importance of establishing strong writing skills.

We would also like to extend our gratitude to our colleagues who contributed to this project in ways too numerous to mention, with particular recognition to: Donald Swanson, Wright State University; Martha Kuchar, Ph.D.; Mert Powell, Ferris State University; Mary Kate Brennan, Bryant and Stratton for their guidance in preparing the manuscript.

ROBERTA ALLEN
MARCIA MASCOLINI

# 1 Think Before You Write

*Writing and problem solving require the same thinking skills. If you can decide which car to buy or class to take, then you can write a good report. This text will show you the way.*

Good writing results from clear thinking. In fact, writing has often been described as "thinking on paper." Understanding writing as a thinking process is an important idea, especially for those who are reluctant to write or who feel they don't write well. Putting writing in a "thinking" perspective helps you overcome writer's block as well as improve the writing itself.

Drafts that you write as you think through a writing problem are simply parts of a larger process. Getting your thoughts down on paper without concern for perfection encourages thinking and analysis. Practiced writers report that writing one idea will lead them to several other ideas, merely as a result of brainstorming on paper. Giving your thoughts a physical form, whether by pen or computer, triggers additional and more developed analysis of a writing problem.

The purpose of this text is to assist you in both your writing and your thinking efforts as you practice writing tasks common to various professions. Writing requires the same skills necessary for critical thinking. For messages to be written clearly, the writer must be able to think clearly too. Each portion of this text is designed to emphasize a particular critical thinking skill and help you apply the skill as you write for a specific purpose. You will find chapters devoted to analyzing information, presenting facts, and persuading a reader. Corresponding writing skills include addressing a specific audience, composing appropriate topic sentences with supporting material, and organizing information according to a specific purpose. Analysis, organization, and evaluation require effective thinking and writing abilities.

As your writing improves, you will find that your understanding of specific applications improves, which will further enhance your writing. You will soon approach writing problems with the confidence gained from applying your critical thinking skills productively.

## Audience Analysis

Your first task is to analyze the writing situation in general terms. What is your purpose and who is your audience? Determining the audience, both primary and secondary, for your message is the critical first step in the thinking–writing cycle. Consider the probable primary reader, the intended receiver of your message. A secondary audience may also exist, perhaps others who will receive copies of your message. For example, an employee who prepares a report for a supervisor should also consider other possible readers or listeners.

Whether the message will be meaningful to your audience depends on a careful analysis of audience needs, expectations, knowledge, and attitudes toward your subject. Imagine the questions that your readers might ask about your message. Anticipate not only their questions, but also their reactions to your responses. Are there parts of the message your audience might resist or accept? Can you estimate your audience's knowledge of the subject? Think about whether your message will be too complicated or too simple for the audience. Analyze your audience as thoroughly as possible before writing.

Here is a summary of key ideas useful for audience analysis:

1. Who is the primary reader? Secondary?
2. What does the audience already know about my subject?
3. What audience characteristics will affect the organization and style of my message? Consider traits such as their role in an organization, cultural norms, and attitudes.
4. What will my audience consider the most important aspects of my message?
5. What are the format preferences of my audience?

Suppose that a college instructor requested a report about microcomputer sales in your city. How would your report differ from one on the same topic requested by your boss on the job? You would need to evaluate each audience's knowledge of the subject, determine the key points that each audience is primarily interested in, consider the physical format that each audience desires, and organize your writing according to these audience expectations.

Your first step, then, in preparing a written message should be to make a simple list of reader characteristics and expectations. Your list for the report on computer sales written for a college instructor might look like this:

*Audience:* College instructor in writing class

*Audience characteristics:* Has indicated experience with the word processing function of one microcomputer model; sophisticated general vocabulary but moderate knowledge of computer jargon.

*Audience expectations:* Is primarily interested in secondary research results concerning microcomputer use among different population types; is expecting a term paper format, including report headings and full documentation of secondary sources.

A report on the same general topic prepared for your job supervisor would differ in both purpose and content.

*Audience:* Job supervisor at office supplies company

*Audience characteristics:* Has years of experience with the office functions of several microcomputer models; has knowledge of programming languages; is familiar with technical computer jargon but prefers simple and clear vocabulary in reports; is interested in the microcomputer model distribution in a sales region currently under study for possible markets of office supplies.

*Audience expectations:* Is expecting a short memo report format that highlights only key ideas and that is easy to read.

As you can see from these thumbnail audience sketches, the report for each audience will have a different purpose, be written in different styles with different computer terms, and have different physical formats. To give each audience the kind of report that is most meaningful, you have to consider all these audience traits and audience needs. Jotting down a simple list, neither long nor complicated, will be very useful as you think about the written message, plan it, and finally write it.

When you don't know your audience well enough to make a list of audience traits, you may have to rely on instinct or informed guessing. If you are careful not to allow bias or prejudice to affect your idea of the audience, then you are usually safe in making some conservative judgments about the audience. For instance, it may be safe to assume that an unknown audience would prefer concrete, simple language rather than abstract, complex language in a report. It would not be safe to assume that an unknown audience would react to humorous material in the same way you would. Therefore, if you are unable to list specific audience characteristics, list general and widely accepted reader characteristics such as "will prefer simple language" or "will prefer to see graphs instead of paragraphs full of numbers."

## Purpose and Form

Academic assignments, such as papers and essays requested by your instructors, are requested in the same way that work supervisors request reports and other information from their employees. Written messages that someone else asks for are called *reader-initiated messages;* messages that you decide to write yourself are *writer-initiated.*

When someone requests a written message, you are more easily able to determine the purpose and form. Follow the directions very closely when a report or other message is requested. You may need to ask for a more detailed explanation. A good idea for both students and employees is to write a simple sentence stating the purpose of the message as you understand it. Then present the statement to the person requesting the report for verification. Making sure that you are on the right track from the very beginning will often save time, and avoid confusion or a negative reaction to your report later on.

### General Purposes for Writing

General purposes for writing both in schools and on jobs include the following:

- To report research results
- To provide an opinion
- To summarize information
- To show comparisons/contrasts
- To describe
- To define
- To show how something works
- To give directions
- To persuade or sell

Both reader- and writer-initiated messages can accomplish these purposes. Matching an appropriate organizational pattern to understanding the specific purpose for a specific audience is your first prewriting goal.

The format, or physical appearance, of the message also needs to be agreed on before you begin writing. If the person requesting the message does not specify a particular format, you should always ask. Instructors will usually be quite specific about what the report should look like. To determine a report format for nonacademic assignments, you could find reports in office files to use as models or consult texts and reference manuals for common styles. You will begin to see that the format of a message depends on both its purpose, or content, and on the preferred format of the audience.

The most popular formats for written messages in schools are paragraphs, essays, research papers, letters, and memos. Formats most often used at work are memos, short reports, letters, and short responses on printed forms. (See Appendix A for memo and letter formats.)

## Summary

Thinking about purpose, audience, and format is an important part of the prewriting process. Once you have mastered this process, you will automatically ask these questions when placed in a writing situation:

- Who requested this message?
- What do I know about my audience?
- What does my audience expect to see?
- In what format does the audience wish to see it?

Answers to these questions will be useful as you begin to think about the information your message will contain, which is the subject of the next chapter. Before reading further, think about some of the problems in the following exercises. Practice your ability to understand different audiences as you work through these exercises.

## EXERCISES

1. Here is a list of some common writing situations. For each writing task, determine the message's primary purpose and list some audience features. What will the audience expect to see in writing? What format will the audience prefer?

   *Situation One*

   Having just enrolled in a business marketing class, you learn that a research paper is required, due in seven weeks, on a topic of your choice.

   *General purpose:* From the list of general purposes for writing on page 5, choose "to report research results."

   ______________________________

   ______________________________

   *Specific purpose:* ______________________________

   ______________________________

   Audience characteristics (include reader interest, knowledge, vocabulary, attitude): ______________________________

   ______________________________

   *Audience expectations* (include what the audience wants to know or see in this writing): ______________________________

   ______________________________

   *Format specifications* (how does the audience want to see it?):

   ______________________________

   ______________________________

   *Situation Two*

   You must provide your wealthy aunt with a written justification for the $5,000 she is willing to give you for college expenses.

   *General purpose:* ______________________________

   ______________________________

   *Specific purpose:* ______________________________

   ______________________________

*Audience characteristics:* ______________________________

______________________________________________

*Audience expectations:* ______________________________

______________________________________________

F*ormat specifications:* ______________________________

______________________________________________

*Situation Three*

Your college writing instructor has requested a paper detailing your experience in previous writing classes.

*General purpose:* ______________________________

______________________________________________

*Specific purpose:* ______________________________

______________________________________________

*Audience characteristics:* ______________________________

______________________________________________

*Audience expectations:* ______________________________

______________________________________________

*Format specifications:* ______________________________

______________________________________________

*Situation Four*

As an employee at the local convenience store, you decide to write to your boss about a security plan you've designed.

*General purpose:* ______________________________

______________________________________________

*Specific purpose:* ______________________________

______________________________________________

*Audience characteristics:* ______________________________

______________________________________________

*Audience expectations:* ______________________________

______________________________________________

*Format specifications:* ______________________________

______________________________________________

*Situation Five*

As an editor of a company newsletter, you want to ask for possible items from other employees for publication.

*General purpose:* ______________________________

______________________________________________

*Specific purpose:* ______________________________

______________________________________________

*Audience characteristics:* ______________________________

______________________________________________

*Audience expectations:* ______________________________

______________________________________________

*Format specifications:* ______________________________

______________________________________________

2. Terry Crayton, a newly hired marketing analyst for Nature's Foods, received instructions by phone from her supervisor, Chris Angel, to write a short report on the Chicago frozen yogurt market. The supervisor was rushed and didn't give Terry many details. Chris told Terry to contact the office manager assistant should questions arise about the project.
   a. What special problems might Terry encounter in preparing the first report for Chris?

      ______________________________________________

      ______________________________________________

      ______________________________________________

   b. What information needs to be in the report?

      ______________________________________________

      ______________________________________________

      ______________________________________________

c. Do you have any advice in deciding on a format?

d. Are there secondary audiences for this report?

3. Secure a dictionary or encyclopedia written for children. Compare definitions for the same words or topics to those in a dictionary or encyclopedia written for adult audiences. Choose ten words or topics. Make a two-column chart showing the comparisons. In the first column, write the definition of the word or topic written for children. In the second column, write the definition of the same word or topic written for adults. Then write a short description of the major differences in language and ideas.

4. Write a description of the ways to score points in American football. Rewrite this description for a visitor from a foreign country who has never seen an American football game. What changes were necessary for the international audience?

5. With an international audience (people for whom English is a second language) in mind, write instructions for the following processes:

   Applying for a driver's license

   Using a self-serve gasoline pump

Borrowing a book from a library

______________________________________________

______________________________________________

______________________________________________

______________________________________________

______________________________________________

______________________________________________

Requesting telephone service

______________________________________________

______________________________________________

______________________________________________

______________________________________________

______________________________________________

______________________________________________

Figuring a tip for a restaurant server

______________________________________________

______________________________________________

______________________________________________

______________________________________________

______________________________________________

______________________________________________

6. A few of the following words have appeared throughout this chapter. Check your dictionary to verify their meanings. Write a definition for each word with different audiences in mind: a child in elementary school, a speaker of English as a second language, a college student.

   Bias ______________________________________

   Concrete __________________________________

   Conservative ______________________________

Corresponding ______________________________

Critical ______________________________

Empathy ______________________________

Enhance ______________________________

Expectations ______________________________

Format ______________________________

Initiate ______________________________

Justification ______________________________

Moderate ______________________________

Portion ______________________________

Sketch ______________________________

Thumbnail ______________________________

Verify ______________________________

Word processing ______________________________

7. Save your mail until you have accumulated ten pieces. Make a list of the items you received. State the general purpose and the specific purpose of each piece of mail.

| | |
|---|---|
| 1. ____________________ | 6. ____________________ |
| 2. ____________________ | 7. ____________________ |
| 3. ____________________ | 8. ____________________ |
| 4. ____________________ | 9. ____________________ |
| 5. ____________________ | 10. ____________________ |

In addressing you as the primary reader, did the writer analyze your needs and wants correctly? (That is, did you respond to each piece of mail as the writer wished? Explain why you did or did not.)

Organize your answer as a chart similar to the following form.

| *Mail Item* | *General Purpose* | *Specific Purpose* | *Response* |
|---|---|---|---|
| | | | |
| | | | |
| | | | |
| | | | |
| | | | |
| | | | |
| | | | |
| | | | |
| | | | |
| | | | |

# 2 Generate and Organize Information

*If you could draw your own thinking process, would the picture be in loops or a straight line? Both maps for loopers (page 19) and outlines for linear thinkers (page 22) can help generate ideas and organize them.*

After analyzing your audience, determining the purpose for your message, and thinking about the form of your message, you are ready to begin gathering ideas. Several techniques explained in the first part of this chapter will help you generate these ideas. In the second part of the chapter, you will work on organizing your ideas in outline form.

## Techniques for Generating Ideas

The three techniques that we will look at as ways to help you develop ideas for your messages are brainstorming, mapping, and freewriting. Some of them will work better for you than others, and some will work better for certain topics than others. Try all of them to see which ones work best for you.

#### Brainstorming

Brainstorming is one of the most useful and popular techniques for producing ideas. You may use it when you are working with others in a group or when you are working alone. Whichever way you use it, following a few guidelines will help you get the most out of the activity.

- Focus on your topic without interruption for 10–15 minutes.
- Jot down every idea that occurs to you.
- Don't stop to make corrections.
- Jot down ideas in whatever form they occur to you—as a single word, phrase, question, or sentence.
- Don't criticize your own ideas or the ideas of those you may be working with.
- Try to write down as many ideas as possible, even if some of them seem only remotely connected with your topic.

Here is a list of ideas that resulted from one student's brainstorming session. His instructor assigned a short report to be written on some aspect of energy conservation. Having determined the purpose of his report to be *informational* and his audience to be a *college instructor,* he then decided to limit his topic to home energy conservation. As you read through his list, note his thought processes. One idea led to another, which often led to another. Ideas will multiply when you allow yourself to brainstorm a topic in the prewriting stage.

> *Purpose of report:* To provide information about home energy conservation.
>
> *Format to keep in mind:* Five pages, essay style.
>
> *Audience:* Informed instructor who is interested in "how-to" information and practical tips for homeowners; instructor also expresses strong energy conservation values.

*List of items:*

heat
power companies
cold weather
caulking
electricity vs. gas
lights
living habits in America
air conditioning
climate
microwaves
refrigerators
window kits
heat loss analysis
solar energy
coats
sun belt
furnace emissions
oil vs. gas and electricity
bulb life
68° in winter
insulation
hot water
appliances
showers vs. tub baths
greenhouses

When you have your unedited, uncensored list of ideas, you are ready to evaluate your list. Some ways to evaluate your ideas are to:

- Cross out duplicate ideas.
- Reword ideas for the clearest expression.
- Discuss each idea.
- Add other ideas that occur to you as you review your list.
- Combine two or more similar ideas.
- Select your best ideas.
- Rank-order your ideas: Put the best one first, the second best second, etc., to the end of your list.

#### Mapping

Mapping is another technique often used to generate ideas. Mapping enables you to visualize your ideas as they grow from your topic and helps you group similar ideas. To map your ideas, begin by putting your topic in a circle in the center of a sheet of paper. See Figure 2-1. Then draw a line from the circle and write an idea that represents one aspect of your topic. Put that idea in a circle. Think of as many points related to the idea as you can, drawing lines and circles as appropriate. Figure 2-1 shows a map that a student drew to generate ideas about her career in accounting. She has decided that she wishes to work for a major accounting firm, thus narrowing her topic to within workable limits.

### Freewriting

Freewriting is a third technique to help you focus your ideas. Few things are more frustrating for a writer than staring at a blank sheet of paper or computer monitor. Set yourself a goal of ten minutes to begin with. During those ten minutes, write down everything you can think of to say about your subject. Don't stop writing. If you feel you've run out of ideas, write "I don't know what to write" until a new idea on your subject occurs to you. Don't stop to review, cross out, or correct. At the end of the ten minutes, go back to see what you've said. Some parts of what you've written you'll discard immediately. Underline or save sentences that capture ideas that you can build on for your report.

A student decided to write on the subject of exercise. Here is what she produced in ten minutes.

> Exercise is something I should do more of. Everybody should probably exercise more. The only problem with exercising is that it is boring. You pay a big fee to a health club and then think of the fourteen reasons you can't go to exercise that night. You just had your hair done and don't want to get it wet. You don't feel well. You want to watch TV or go shopping or clean your closet. You have homework to do. You don't want to go alone. The health club is too far away or it's too hot out or it's too cold out. Your exercise clothes are dirty or they're clean and you don't want to get them dirty. You'll do it tomorrow. You won't exercise, but instead you'll skip dessert. Exercise doesn't help you lose weight anyway. After you exercise, you have a big appetite. People at the health club using passive equipment and talking about going for a pizza after they're finished. What can you do to make it less boring? Go with a friend? Exercise at home so that you won't have to make a special trip out? What will motivate me to exercise at home? I can listen to music. I can time myself to the length of various tapes. Watch

**Figure 2-1.** Mapping your ideas.

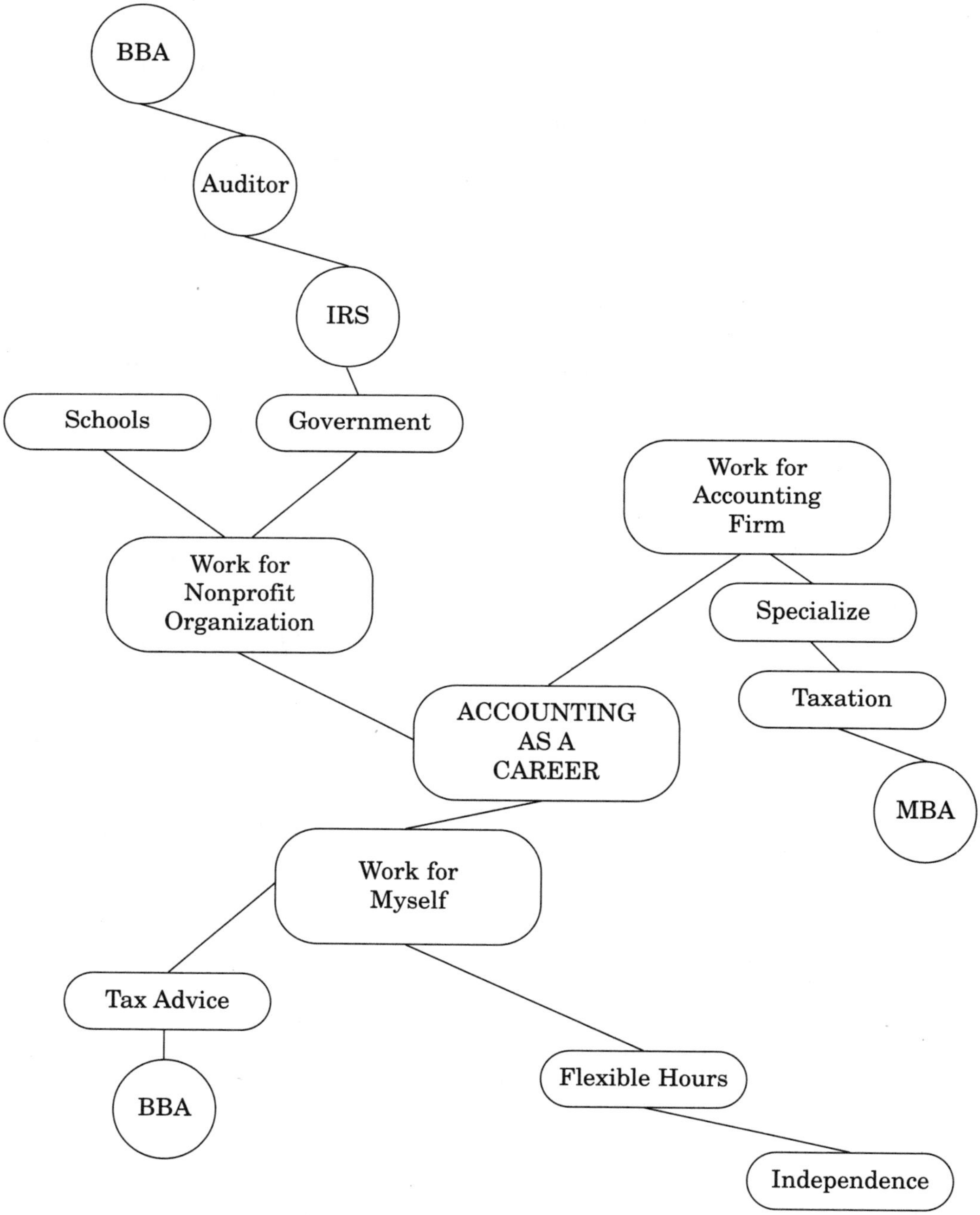

> TV. Do sit-ups to Dan Rather. Maybe buy some exercise equipment. What kind? Rowing machine? Exercise bike? Tummy depressor? This sounds as if it could be as expensive as joining a health club. I could buy a whole bunch of equipment and still not exercise like my brother-in-law. He has a home exercise museum in his basement. You can follow every fad that has come out in the last 10–15 years. And the best part is all of the equipment is in mint condition.... (Time is up.)

After rereading what she has written, the student has some ideas that she can use in a paper. She thinks she knows enough to write about avoiding boredom while exercising. She can also write about trends in exercise equipment. Perhaps she can find out what her school offers students who want to exercise and compare the school's facilities to those of a health club. Another possibility is to write about the kinds of exercises a person can do without buying a lot of expensive equipment.

## Outlining

After you've gathered a list of ideas on a topic, you are ready to take the next step: organizing your ideas. Preparing an outline is a useful organizational technique. Outlining helps you plan an effective message that your readers can grasp easily. It also shows you your ideas as a whole and gives you the opportunity, before writing, of rearranging your ideas—putting them in a form that best meets your reader's needs for information. Additionally, studying your outline will reveal gaps where you need to add material as well as material that overlaps or is off the point.

### Organizing Information

Outlining is the process of organizing a list of ideas. Your first task is to remove all items not related to the main topic. Does the item support, describe, or provide an example of your main idea? If not, delete the idea.

Your second task in developing an outline is to group the remaining items according to subtopics. Understanding the movement from general to specific is extremely important in this step. The most general items can serve as categories for more specific items. These specific items may themselves serve as smaller categories for even more specific items. After reading these three steps, study the example that follows.

1. Determine the most general, or primary, items on the list. These are subtopics in relation to your main idea. They typically answer the questions *why* and *how* concerning your topic.
2. Sort items that belong under each subtopic. Place them under appropriate subtopics.
3. Identify items that are even more specific and list them under the subtopics you identified in step 2.

### Example of a Three-Step Outline

Outlining begins with ideas such as the following brainstorming list for the topic "Working as an Air Traffic Controller."

| | |
|---|---|
| Training | Biannual raises |
| High demand in the 1990s through 2000 | College degree in aviation systems |
| $30,000 starting salary | Tracking commercial and private aircraft |
| Communicating ground control information to pilots | Two-year Navy program |
| Salary expectations | Routing aircraft in both normal and emergency situations |
| Four-year Air Force program for enlisted personnel | Military training |

After developing the list of ideas, we can begin grouping similar ideas into categories. Here is how such a grouping would look:

*Group I*

Training

Two-year internship

Military training

Four-year Air Force program for enlisted personnel
College degree in aviation systems
Two-year Navy program
Civilian training

*Group II*

$30,000 starting salary
Salary expectations
Biannual raises

*Group III*

Communicating ground control information to pilots
Tracking commercial and private aircraft
Routing aircraft in both normal and emergency situations

By grouping ideas, we can tell we have three primary subtopics. We can name the first two subtopics "Training" (I) and "Salary expectations" (II). What name is appropriate for the third subtopic? Because all items in that category relate to what an air traffic controller does on the job, we can call it "Job responsibilities" (III).

After determining the primary subtopics in each category, we can go to step 2: sorting specific examples into subtopic categories. Under "Training," two more subtopics emerge: "Civilian training" and "Military training." Even more specific items may be subordinated to these subtopics to produce a category with these subdivisions:

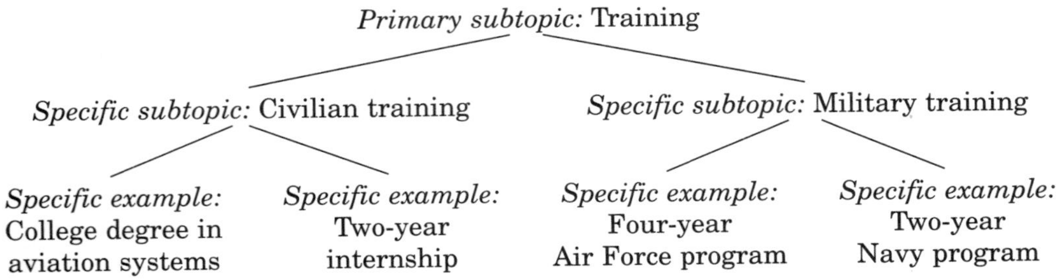

To move beyond the informal, branching outline like this one, we can assign formal numbers and letters to all items to produce a formal outline.

1. All *primary subtopics* have capital roman numeral labels: I, II, III, IV, V, etc.
2. All *specific subtopics* under each primary subtopic have capital letter labels: A, B, C, D, E, etc.
3. All *specific examples,* which come under specific subtopics, have arabic numeral labels: 1, 2, 3, 4, 5, etc.

The finished outline for the topic "Working as an Air Traffic Controller" should look like this:

**I.** Training
  A. Military
    1. Four-year Air Force program for enlisted personnel
    2. Two-year Navy program
  B. Civilian
    1. College degree in aviation systems
    2. Two-year internship
**II.** Salary expectations
  A. $30,000 starting salary
  B. Biannual raises
**III.** Job responsibilities
  A. Communicating ground control information to pilots
  B. Tracking aircraft
    1. Commercial
    2. Private
  C. Routing aircraft
    1. Normal situations
    2. Emergency situations

### Using Outline Logic

As you move from a general idea to a specific example, be sure that your subtopics are parallel in structure and importance.

To show parallel structure, subtopics and supports should display vertical logic. In the preceding example, items I, II, and III are all primary subtopics that are equal to each other in importance. They are all noun phrases, and they share a similar relationship to the topic, "Working as an Air Traffic Controller." The specific subtopics that support the primary subtopics are also parallel and have the same degree of specificity. The same is true of the specific examples.

Vertical logic also requires that each item in the outline is subordinated properly. That is, A should be a subordinate idea to I, and 1 should be a subordinate idea to A. Note the following subordination of ideas under the primary subtopic "Energy conservation":

**I.** Energy conservation
  A. Solar energy
    1. Residential uses
    2. Commercial uses
  B. Nuclear power

A and B are subsets of I; 1 and 2 are subsets of A. Every division logically has two parts because an item may not be divided into one part, just as an apple cannot be divided into only one half. Thus, remember, if you make a division, two or more subsets must result from it. For example, if "2. Commercial uses" were to be divided, the subsets developed might look like this:

2. Commercial uses
  a. Factory
  b. Office
  c. Store

## Summary

You can use techniques such as brainstorming, mapping, and freewriting to produce ideas. Once you have a set of ideas, you are ready to organize them in an outline. Outline logic is one of the most useful organizational concepts you will learn. Understanding the parallel structure of outlined ideas allows you to develop, organize, and write messages of all kinds. Additionally, well organized outlines reflect two important qualities: ideas are parallel at similar stages and specific ideas are subordinated, or put beneath, more general ideas. In an outline, all capital letter items—A, B, C, etc.—are alike in content and relationship to major roman numeral ideas—I, II, III, etc. The items are also written in parallel, or similar, grammatical form. For example, all roman numeral items might be nouns or noun phrases, or they might be verbs or verb phrases like "Analyze the audience," "Develop an outline," "Write a paragraph." Capital letter items, arabic number items, and other subordinated items are also parallel.

## EXERCISES

1. Apply each of the techniques (brainstorming, mapping, and freewriting) for generating ideas to one or more of these ideas. (Use extra sheets of paper, if necessary.)

   Selecting a long-distance telephone service

   Selecting a major household appliance

   Benefits of recycling waste products

   Developments in laser technology

   Investment opportunities under $1,000

   A description of the city government structure

   Personal characteristics that qualify you for a specific job:

   Books you own

   Cereals on the market

   Economic systems

   Types of schools

   Historical eras in the United States

   Food on hand in your house

   Cars on the market

   Courses offered at your school

   Magazines in circulation

   Types of government

   Clothing you own

   Types of fuel

2. Arrange items in these brainstormed lists in logically organized outlines. Use the outline designs provided.

*Outline A*

| | |
|---|---|
| Availability | 12 miles per gallon–city |
| $25,000 base price | Corvette |
| Price | October new model unveiling |
| 20 miles per gallon–highway | $30,000 with options |
| Factory deliveries monthly | Fuel consumption |

**I.** ________________________________

A. ______________________________

1. ____________________________
2. ____________________________

B. ______________________________

1. ____________________________
2. ____________________________

C. ______________________________

1. ____________________________
2. ____________________________

*Outline B*

| | |
|---|---|
| Researching skills | Recommends stock purchases |
| Studies market | Critical thinking skills |
| Holds seminars for clients | Investigates businesses |
| Skills required of stockbrokers | Telephones clients |
| Public relations skills | Writes sales letters |
| Recommends other investments | |

**I.** ________________________________

A. ______________________________

1. ____________________________
2. ____________________________
3. ____________________________

B. ________________________________

1. ________________________________

2. ________________________________

C. ________________________________

1. ________________________________

2. ________________________________

*Outline C*

Morning schedule preferred
Business core requirements
East campus location first choice
Class location
Requirements for classes
No Friday classes
Downtown campus second choice
Criteria for selecting courses
Time of class
Humanities requirements
Physical education requirements

**I.** ________________________________

A. ________________________________

1. ________________________________

2. ________________________________

B. ________________________________

1. ________________________________

2. ________________________________

3. ________________________________

C. ________________________________

1. ________________________________

2. ________________________________

3. Try the remaining exercises without an outline skeleton provided for you.

*Outline A*

Dorm fee includes meals.

Dorm is near classes.

Dorm has little closet space.

A comparison of dorm and apartment living.

Apartments have more storage space than dorms.

Dorm space is smaller than apartment space.

Apartment rent is cheaper than dorm.

Overall, a dorm is cheaper than an apartment.

Travel to classes from apartment is costly.

Dorm is located more conveniently.

Campus facilities are near dorm.

______________________________________________

______________________________________________

______________________________________________

______________________________________________

______________________________________________

______________________________________________

______________________________________________

______________________________________________

______________________________________________

______________________________________________

______________________________________________

______________________________________________

______________________________________________

______________________________________________

______________________________________________

______________________________________________

*Outline B*

Columbia Broadcasting System

30-minute network evening news

*USA Today*

Television

American Broadcasting Company

Radio

City-based newspapers

*Chicago Tribune*

*The Wall Street Journal*

Papers with national circulation

News media available to U.S. citizens

24-hour cable news service

Hourly news and weather

AM and FM selections

*Denver Post*

National Broadcasting Corporation

Newspapers

*Outline C*

Listed in *Fortune 500*

In-house training for employees

Consumer appeal growing

Managers use participatory styles

More fiber in cereals

Encourage worker input in decisions

Personnel policies encourage production

Kellogg Company is a sound investment

Steady increases in net sales annually

Less sugar in products

Seminars in writing and fitness

________________________________________

________________________________________

________________________________________

________________________________________

________________________________________

________________________________________

________________________________________

________________________________________

________________________________________

________________________________________

________________________________________

4. Use the ideas for one of the topics you generated in Exercise 1 to organize an outline.

5. Using your dictionary, write definitions for the following words:

   Abstraction ______________________________

   Censor ______________________________

   Civilian ______________________________

   Conservation ______________________________

   Delete ______________________________

   Generate ______________________________

   Irrelevant ______________________________

   Parallel ______________________________

   Potential ______________________________

   Remote ______________________________

   Subordinate ______________________________

   Vertical ______________________________

# 3 Compose Paragraphs for Specific Purposes

*The paragraph is the basic building block for all messages, whether you're writing a job application letter or newspaper article.*

A paragraph is the basic unit of most practical writing, both at school and at work. Paragraphs are composed of sentences about a single idea. They may stand alone as a single message or be combined with other paragraphs to form a larger unit, such as a report or essay. Working with a single paragraph as a unit of writing makes a lot of sense for beginning practical writers.

Three basic rules for writing effective paragraphs for any practical purpose are to compose a precise topic sentence, to show how the supporting sentences relate to the topic, and to arrange the supporting sentences in a logical way. This chapter covers these three rules. Stated in other words, paragraphs must display:

1. A precise, limited topic sentence.
2. Unity of support (related supporting sentences).
3. Coherent support (logically organized sentences).

**Focused Topic Sentences**

Practical paragraphs begin with a clear statement of the writer's purpose. Business, technical, and most academic writing assignments include these purposes:

- Memos and reports providing information to employees or an audience requesting them
- Descriptions of processes and instructions
- Analyses of problems and solutions
- Evaluations
- Short answer and essay responses on tests
- Papers and reports for courses

Your reader should know the exact purpose of your paragraph after reading the first sentence.

Leading into a subject with general, vague sentences is an error many beginning writers make. For some, a broadly stated opening sentence seems comforting. Covering all possible interpretations has been a safe approach for them in grammar and secondary schools. Using words without precise meanings, such as "society," "man," "world," "today," "a lot," and "many" in the topic sentence should be avoided, not preferred.

The topic sentence must introduce a focused limited subject. A meaningful topic sentence communicates a single idea in concrete and specific language. Instead of "a lot," write "75 percent of sales." Instead of "business world today," write "manufacturing companies." Putting subjects in language that brings real, physical images to the audience's mind takes practice. To begin, write some possible topic sentences given general categories. Go over your list a second time and refine the topic sentences further. Avoid general words, especially "a lot," "many," "today," and "world." Also beware of absolute words and phrases such as "every," "all," "always," and "never."

Here is an example of a general topic, computer technology, that the writer has thought about and refined.

| | |
|---|---|
| *General topic:* | Computer technology is everywhere. |
| *Possible topic:* | Computer technology has changed libraries. |
| *Refined topic:* | Computer technology has improved the quality of service to patrons. |

Here is another example of a general topic that the writer has refined. Notice how the more general "Great Lakes" has become the more specific "Lake Michigan" and how "polluted" has become "toxic chemicals."

| | |
|---|---|
| *General topic:* | The Great Lakes are polluted. |
| *Possible topic:* | Lake Michigan is polluted. |
| *Refined topic:* | Lake Michigan contains hazardous amounts of toxic chemicals. |

Refining topic sentences is easier when you have organized your ideas in outline form. You can use subtopics or categories already in place to provide specific language for the topic sentence. Because your subtopics answer the questions why and how about the topic, they are the best words or phrases for limiting the subject. Consider again the outline about air traffic controllers:

*Purpose:* To describe a job as an air traffic controller (ATC)

**I.** Training required for ATCs

- A. College degree/aviation systems
- B. Two-year internship/apprenticeship

**II.** Job responsibilities

- A. Tracking aircraft in corridors—radar and visual
- B. Communicating information to pilots
- C. Routing aircraft—routine and nonroutine

**III.** Salary expectations
- A. Market conditions, starting salaries in 199X
- B. Promotions and raises, typical ranks

**IV.** Job outlook in next decade
- A. Demand in period 1990–2000 by region
- B. Effects of deregulation and union changes

Your topic can include the specific ideas "air traffic controller, training, responsibilities, salary, and occupational outlook." Your main idea of the topic sentence includes the phrase "air traffic controller." Put in single-word, parallel form, the subtopics are "training," "responsibilities," "salary," and "outlook."

You will begin to think of ideas for your topic sentence depending on the purpose, audience, or point of view of the paragraph. This topic sentence would suit a specific audience needing a purely descriptive paragraph: "Here is the information you requested about the air traffic controller position."

For an informative purpose to a general audience, this is appropriate: "An air traffic controller's training, responsibilities, salary, and employment outlook have changed over the past 20 years."

And for an opinion to a general audience, the following might be written: "Because of the rising demand, increased salaries, excellent training, and serious responsibilities, I have chosen to become an air traffic controller."

Note that each topic sentence gives a slightly different point of view of the subject. Which view do you want to emphasize to your audience? Here are some choices to make a topic sentence work for you:

- To communicate information
- To communicate an opinion
- To provide subtopics in advance to guide your audience to what you are going to say in the rest of the paragraph
- To give the reader a clue about the organization of the paragraph: Compare/contrast? Develop by examples? Develop by enumerating, or listing, important points? A process description?

### Unify Supporting Sentences

A paragraph is unified if all subtopics and supporting sentences relate directly to the topic sentence. Off-subject ideas, stray examples, and irrelevant facts destroy paragraph unity. Following a well organized outline lessens the chance of including sentences that do not belong. As a child you probably played picture games requiring you to identify the object that didn't belong in a group. You were able to show that a pictured orange vegetable did not belong in a group of green vegetables. The principle of paragraph unity is really no different. Each sentence's meaning must clearly answer the questions why, how, what, or where about the topic sentence.

Consider the following topic sentence:

> Cats make excellent house pets for working people.

Supports should answer the question why. A good mental reminder is to imagine the word *because* at the beginning of each supporting subtopic. Your specific supporting sentences for subtopics would provide clear examples of your "because" sentences.

> (because) Cats can remain indoors indefinitely.
> —the advantage of Kitty Litter
>
> (because) Cats prefer to entertain themselves.
> —the story of Tiger and his love of Kleenex

If you are able to link each sentence in your paragraph, both subtopics and specific supports, to the topic sentence, you have achieved paragraph unity.

### Coherence

*Coherence* means logically connected. Supporting sentences must be organized in a logical and meaningful pattern to be understood by your reader. A coherent paragraph makes sense to the audience. Ideas show controlled order, and cue words channel thoughts in a particular direction. Each sentence's relationship to the topic sentence is clear.

An ability to empathize with your audience improves coherence. Imagine what questions the reader might ask and in what order information might be expected. Because you have anticipated a reader's response to each idea and supporting sentence, you are then able to provide cue words, or transitions, so that logical connections are made. Transitions mirror thought processes. They provide the link between ideas and sentences. Here are some common transitions and their purposes:

- *To show a transition to a supporting example:* For example, such as, for instance.
- *To show cause and effect:* Consequently, therefore, so, as a result, then.
- *To show addition or emphasis:* Moreover, furthermore, as well as, also, in addition, another, other.
- *To show opposite, contrast:* However, though, on the other hand, although.
- *To show order or time:* First, second, third; next, now, then, last, finally.

You should choose transition words carefully and use them sparingly. Beginning every sentence with a cue word clutters a paragraph with unnecessary words. Gentle guidance for the reader remains an important goal.

From a list of brainstormed ideas, this writer composed a paragraph about studying in dormitories. She added transitions to improve coherence.

*List*

| | |
|---|---|
| Distractions while studying | Invitations to party |
| High noise level | Blasting stereos |
| Talking roommates | Phone ringing |
| Games available in lounge | Ping pong, video games, pool |

*Outline*

Studying in a dormitory is difficult for beginning students.

**I.** The noise level is high.

A. Stereo noise

B. Phone ringing

**II.** Roommates distract me.
  A. Invitations to party
  B. Roommates' desire to talk
**III.** The game room is temptation.
  A. Pool
  B. Ping pong
  C. Video games

*Paragraph*

Since becoming a college freshman, I've learned that studying in a dormitory is difficult. One reason is the extremely high noise level. Although quiet hours are in effect between 7:00 and 11:00 P.M., students still blast hard rock stereo music at a thousand decibels. Phones ring constantly, adding to the ruckus. Other distractions include my roommates' invitations to parties and gab sessions. Making new friends and learning what they think about Professor Smith or the math requirement is much more interesting than the accounting problems due tomorrow. Finally, the dormitory lounge, with its cozy atmosphere and entertaining games, is a temptation each evening. Pool, ping pong, and video games are available 24 hours a day. Tuning out the noise, saying no to roommates' invitations, and ignoring the game room would improve my efforts to study in Washington Hall.

### Putting Writing into Perspective

Research about writing and thinking shows that writers learn more by writing on subjects that interest them or that are in their major fields of study, such as engineering, business, or art. Not only are beginning writers more likely to be interested in the subjects themselves, but they see the value of learning the "conventions," or special characteristics of writing in specific areas. For example, students majoring in sociology will learn not only the language of sociology, but also the writing style and organization of research reports. Students' own writing will improve as they become familiar with writing in sociology. The same is true of all disciplines. Accounting majors begin to think and write like practicing accountants if allowed to write about accounting. When your subject and audience become the focus of your writing—and not the *writing* alone—you will notice improved organization, more meaningful sentences, and a clarity of purpose.

Unless your career involves professional writing, becoming a good writer should not necessarily be your objective. Instead, focus on becoming a good engineer, sociologist, or accountant, whose good writing contributes to career success. Writing well enhances any career because you will often be judged by what you write or how you write it. Clear, meaningful, organized writing will improve your professional performance. Demystifying writing, or taking the mystery out of it, is one of the purposes of this text. View practical writing as a tool to help you in your school or working worlds. Think before you write, practice the kinds of writing expected of you (learn the conventions in your field), and practice the principles of good writing introduced here.

## Cases

Case studies in different subject areas can provide writing practice. Producing a paragraph in response to each of the writing situations requires problem solving, audience analysis, and basic organizational skills. A case study encourages a writer to analyze information in a given subject area, such as biology or aviation technology. Several content areas appear in case studies at the end of the chapter, but you may want to create your own case study in a specific subject not included. Posing your own writing problems stimulates thinking as well.

These case studies are "open-ended." They have no one correct solution. Writing on the job is much the same. Often, there are no correct models; instead of a correct answer to a problem, there may be alternatives or choices. You make the decisions, declare a purpose, and communicate your response clearly. Provide any additional information or facts that you believe would improve your response. Most of the case studies can be altered to fit a more specific topic if you want to tailor the purpose to your needs. Be creative as you think about the material given.

On the next page is a checklist that students find helpful as a guide in responding to cases. Although determining the audience appears as the first step in the checklist, determining purpose might be first sometimes. Often they are determined together. Just as cases are open-ended, steps in the writing process must be flexible.

## Summary

Paragraphs are the basic units of writing. Practical writers begin their paragraphs with focused topic sentences to let busy readers know exactly what they are writing about. The topic announced in the topic sentences is often separated into subtopics in the body of the paragraph and always supported by ideas, facts, or examples. These supporting statements must relate to the topic sentence to give the paragraph unity. Paragraphs must also be coherent. Sentences must be organized in anticipation of the reader's need for information.

## CASE ANALYSIS AND RESPONSE CHECKLIST

1. Determine your audience(s).
2. Determine the purpose of writing to this audience.
3. List the main points you need to communicate to the audience.
   Use whatever information is given.
   Brainstorm, map, or freewrite to generate more ideas.
   Gather additional information.
4. Organize the information in a logical outline:
   Are the main points in subtopic positions?
   Do you have specific facts and examples as supports?
   Are all ideas parallel?
5. Convert the outline into a paragraph, checking for unity and coherence.
6. Edit sentences for errors in grammar, mechanics, and spelling.
7. Proofread your finished message carefully.

*A suggestion:* Before submitting a paragraph or outline to be analyzed and evaluated by a trained writer, your instructor, you may find that a peer evaluation session is valuable. Ask another student, co-worker, or friend to read your paper and provide constructive criticism to be used for improving the paragraphs. The checklist makes an excellent peer evaluation form. Use a dictionary or grammar/usage handbook for reference.

## PARAGRAPH SCORE SHEET

5=Excellent    4=Good    3=Average    2=Weak    1=Poor    0=Failure

| | |
|---|---|
| *Content* | |
| Quality of ideas (interesting, amusing, original) | 5 4 3 2 1 0 |
| Development of ideas (details, examples) | 5 4 3 2 1 0 |
| Sufficient specific ideas | 5 4 3 2 1 0 |
| *Structure* | |
| Topic sentence: | |
| Appears as the first sentence in the paragraph. | 5 4 3 2 1 0 |
| Narrows/refines the general topic. | 5 4 3 2 1 0 |
| Expresses the main idea of the paragraph. | 5 4 3 2 1 0 |
| Supporting sentences relate to the idea expressed in the topic sentence (unity). | 5 4 3 2 1 0 |
| *Readability* | |
| Transitions appear where necessary between ideas. | 5 4 3 2 1 0 |
| Grammar | 5 4 3 2 1 0 |
| Word choice | 5 4 3 2 1 0 |
| Punctuation | 5 4 3 2 1 0 |
| Spelling | 5 4 3 2 1 0 |

## EXERCISES

1. Study the following general topics, and use the three-step format to narrow them to refined topics.

   General topic: ______________________

   Possible topic: ______________________

   Refined topic: ______________________

   *General Topics*

   A. Television influences children.

      Possible topic: ______________________

      Refined topic: ______________________

   B. Interest rates declined.

      Possible topic: ______________________

      Refined topic: ______________________

   C. Sunbathing causes skin cancer.

      Possible topic: ______________________

      Refined topic: ______________________

   D. Wildflowers are abundant in North America.

      Possible topic: ______________________

      Refined topic: ______________________

   E. Twentieth-century marriages differ from those in the nineteenth century.

      Possible topic: ______________________

      Refined topic: ______________________

   F. Nuclear energy is important.

      Possible topic: ______________________

      Refined topic: ______________________

   G. Russian politics have changed.

      Possible topic: ______________________

      Refined topic: ______________________

H. Pond life species are interesting.

Possible topic: ______________________________

Refined topic: ______________________________

I. Chicago's architecture shows many styles.

Possible topic: ______________________________

Refined topic: ______________________________

J. Living in a small town is boring.

Possible topic: ______________________________

Refined topic: ______________________________

K. Native Americans deserve more from the government.

Possible topic: ______________________________

Refined topic: ______________________________

2. Reread the student paragraph on p. 39. Underline the transitions used to guide the reader from subtopic to subtopic. Identify the type of transitions used. For example, "Finally" was used to introduce the last, or final, subtopic that named a third reason dorm studying was difficult. After analyzing transitions, explain how the student achieved paragraph unity. Then use the following list of ideas to outline and develop a coherent, unified paragraph. Add any ideas you need to provide more or better examples.

*List*

Articulate speaker

Available Saturdays and weekdays after 1:00

Hours are flexible

Experience in bookkeeping at parent's business

Student majoring in finance

Communicated well in the interview

Recommendation of Jeremy Adams for teller position

*Purpose:* ______________________________

*Intended audience:* ______________________________

*Outline*

Topic sentence: ______________________________

**I.** First subtopic ("Because ...") ______________________

(specific support): ______________________________

(example?) ______________________________

**II.** Second subtopic ("Because ...") ______________________

(specific support): ______________________________

(example?) ______________________________

**III.** Third subtopic ("Because ...") ______________________

(specific support): ______________________________

(example?) ______________________________

Join the topic sentence, subtopics, and specific supports and examples, and provide coherent transitions in composing your paragraph.

______________________________________________

______________________________________________

______________________________________________

______________________________________________

______________________________________________

______________________________________________

______________________________________________

______________________________________________

______________________________________________

______________________________________________

______________________________________________

______________________________________________

______________________________________________

______________________________________________

______________________________________________

______________________________________________

## BUSINESS CASES

1. As a sales trainee for Beta Company, a manufacturer of office furniture, you have been asked by your supervisor to write a brief description of your education and job experience for publication in the company newsletter.

   *Purpose:* ______________________________

   *Audience:* ______________________________

   *Format:* ______________________________

   *Outline*

   ______________________________

   ______________________________

   ______________________________

   ______________________________

   ______________________________

   ______________________________

   ______________________________

   ______________________________

   ______________________________

   ______________________________

   ______________________________

   ______________________________

   ______________________________

   ______________________________

   ______________________________

   ______________________________

   ______________________________

   ______________________________

   ______________________________

   ______________________________

2. You have just begun working for Dixon and Dixon Investment Counseling, a well established firm offering a variety of financial services. As an entry-level stockbroker, you are expected to collect information about companies at the request of potential clients. A client has requested information about the Kellogg Company, the cereal manufacturer in Battle Creek, Michigan. Your supervisor asks you to do some research and provide her with a paragraph of background information to begin her report to the client.

   *Purpose:* ______________________________

   *Audience:* ______________________________

   *Format:* ______________________________

   *Outline*

   ______________________________
   ______________________________
   ______________________________
   ______________________________
   ______________________________
   ______________________________
   ______________________________
   ______________________________
   ______________________________
   ______________________________
   ______________________________
   ______________________________
   ______________________________
   ______________________________
   ______________________________
   ______________________________
   ______________________________
   ______________________________

3. The professor of your marketing class has asked you to write questions for a telephone market survey that will determine the sales potential of Vita (pronounced *veeta,* meaning life), a vitamin-enriched soft drink. In addition to composing the interview questions, you must attach a one-paragraph summary of the survey's purpose.

   *Purpose:* ______________________________

   *Interview questions that satisfy purpose of the case:* ______

   Audience of paragraph: ______________________

   Audience of survey: ______________________

   Paragraph facts: ______________________

4. Each time you travel as a sales representative for Data Corporation, you must submit a brief trip report to your regional manager. The report is a one-paragraph summary describing the purpose, length, and expenses of the trip. Because all trip reports are filed as permanent records, details must be specific, accurate, and verifiable. Write a trip report describing your trip to San Francisco last week.

   *Purpose of paragraph:* ______________________________

   *Audience of paragraph:* ______________________________

   *Subtopics to cover:* ______________________________

   ______________________________________________

   ______________________________________________

   ______________________________________________

   *Supporting facts to include:* ______________________________

   ______________________________________________

   ______________________________________________

   ______________________________________________

   ______________________________________________

   *Outline*

5. Cat Fanciers International is planning its annual convention and has written to you, a customer relations assistant at Fine Hotel in Omaha, Nebraska, for information about your hotel's convention facilities. Bringing the Cat Fanciers to Omaha would mean good business for both the city and the hotel. The first paragraph of your response to the group introduces three good reasons for choosing Fine Hotel for the week-long convention.

   *Purpose of paragraph:* ______________________________

   *Audience(s) of paragraph:* ______________________________

   *Format:* ______________________________

   *Subtopics:* ______________________________

   ______________________________

   ______________________________

   ______________________________

   ______________________________

   ______________________________

   *Supporting details:* ______________________________

   ______________________________

   ______________________________

   ______________________________

   ______________________________

   ______________________________

   *Outline*

## SCIENCE AND TECHNOLOGY CASES

1. The first assignment in your biology class requires classifying and describing the plant life you discovered on a recent hike through the community's nature center. You observed nine types of aquatic (water) plants, trees, and wildflowers. Because this is a beginning research assignment, you do not have to use the plant kingdom classification system but instead are asked to classify them using characteristics you have observed yourself. You have decided that the preceding types (aquatic plants, trees, wildflowers) are good subtopics, or categories, to use. Supply the names of specific plants and trees you noticed and summarize your observations in a paragraph.

   *Purpose:* ______________________________

   *Audience:* ______________________________

   *Subtopics:* ______________________________

   ______________________________

   ______________________________

   ______________________________

   ______________________________

   ______________________________

   *Specific supports:* ______________________________

   ______________________________

   ______________________________

   ______________________________

   ______________________________

   ______________________________

   *Outline*

2. You have been asked to give a short lecture about the basic principles of flight to a group of 30 high school students. In preparing your notes for the presentation, you organize the principles in logical order and explain each. Write the outline for your presentation using these terms you have researched in the library: lift, thrust, propulsion, Newton's third law (for every action there is an opposite and equal reaction), rearward acceleration of air.

   *Purpose:* ______________________________

   *Audience:* ______________________________

   *Library sources on "flight":* ______________________________

   ______________________________

   ______________________________

   ______________________________

   ______________________________

   *Subtopics:* ______________________________

   ______________________________

   ______________________________

   ______________________________

   ______________________________

   ______________________________

   *Outline*

3. The State Department of Natural Resources hired you to work as a summer intern responsible for reporting selective bird counts in your county. You have collected the following information from field workers and must write a one-paragraph memo to your supervisor providing the week's tally. Your report should be organized by species. The number of sightings is given in parentheses.

   7/13–7/19 at Goose Lake: green heron (2); mallard (26); Canada goose (4); belted kingfisher (2); common loon (2)

   7/13–7/19 from plats 1–14: whitebreasted nuthatch (1); yellow-shafted flicker (2); indigo bunting (1)

   7/13–7/19 from baseline to northern shore of Goose Lake: kingfisher (2); mallards (2); yellow-shafted flicker (1); pine siskin (2)

   *Purpose:* ______________________________

   *Audience:* ______________________________

   *Subtopics:* ______________________________

   ______________________________

   ______________________________

   ______________________________

   ______________________________

   ______________________________

   *Specific supports:* ______________________________

   ______________________________

   ______________________________

   ______________________________

   ______________________________

   ______________________________

   *Outline*

4. For your first lab report in chemistry, you must carefully observe and then record your observations of a class demonstration showing the creation of hydrogen and oxygen from water. Here are your notes:

   Form hydrogen and oxygen.

   Use electricity to separate elements.

   Hydrogen and oxygen can be made from water.

   Water is actually two parts hydrogen, one part oxygen.

   Electricity will cause H and O to collect at different poles.

   What instrument may be used to add electric current to water safely?

   *Purpose:* ____________________________________________

   *Audience:* ____________________________________________

   *Order of subtopics in process:* ______________________________

   ____________________________________________________________

   ____________________________________________________________

   ____________________________________________________________

   ____________________________________________________________

   ____________________________________________________________

   ____________________________________________________________

   *Outline*

5. As service manager of Burr Automotive, you have decided to offer reduced rate tuneups to attract new business. Your mailing list contains names of a broad cross section of Salem City's population, your potential customers. However, you can't be sure that everyone will know exactly what a tuneup includes. In a brochure you plan to mail to people on the mailing list, you want to include a brief description of a tuneup that all people can understand.

   *Purpose:* ______________________________

   *Audience:* ______________________________

   *Subtopics to cover:* ______________________________

   ______________________________

   ______________________________

   ______________________________

   ______________________________

   ______________________________

   *Specific supports:* ______________________________

   ______________________________

   ______________________________

   ______________________________

   ______________________________

   ______________________________

   *Outline*

## SOCIAL SCIENCES AND LIBERAL ARTS CASES

1. You plan to apply for a job as camp counselor at Camp Atoma, a special camp for boys and girls who play soccer. The camp is open to children between 8 and 16 years of age. A trained staff provides instruction and recreation to 30 students every two weeks. Summarize your qualifications and interest in the summer job to this prospective employer: Jan Bach, Camp Director.

   *Purpose:* ______________________________

   *Audience:* ______________________________

   *Subtopics:* ______________________________

   ______________________________

   ______________________________

   ______________________________

   ______________________________

   ______________________________

   *Specific supports:* ______________________________

   ______________________________

   ______________________________

   ______________________________

   ______________________________

   ______________________________

   *Outline*

2. As a student teacher of first graders, you must keep a daily journal describing your experiences in three categories: interactions with students, interactions with supervising teacher, and evaluation of instructional methods used by both you and your supervisor. This journal must be submitted to your college adviser at the end of your student teaching experience. Portions will also appear in your written report, which summarizes your activities which is also due to the adviser. Write a journal entry for October 6, a Tuesday, and provide specific descriptions of events in all categories.

   *Purpose:* ______________________________

   *Audience:* ______________________________

   *Subtopics:* ______________________________

   ______________________________

   ______________________________

   ______________________________

   ______________________________

   ______________________________

   *Supporting descriptions:* ______________________________

   ______________________________

   ______________________________

   ______________________________

   ______________________________

   ______________________________

   *Outline*

3. The editor of *The Hilltown Clarion,* a newspaper you've worked for as contributing writer of special features, requests a story on Hilltown's aging population. Younger residents are moving away after high school graduation and tend not to return. Two manufacturers have closed plants. Write an outline of this special feature article for approval before you begin your research.

   *Purpose:* ______________________________

   *Audience:* ______________________________

   *Subtopics:* ______________________________

   ______________________________

   ______________________________

   ______________________________

   ______________________________

   ______________________________

   *Outline*

4. KidCare, a local day care center for children between 2 and 5 years old, is soliciting applications for student aides. As assistant director of the center, you write a job description to be distributed to the Education and Psychology departments at two local colleges. Here is the information you're working with:

   KidCare, Inc., is licensed by state; employs director, assistant director, three teachers; enrollment capacity is 45 per hour; aides needed to assist teachers with group activities, lunches and snacks, story hours, art, field trips, and outdoor activities. Education and psychology students preferred.

   *Purpose:* ______________________________

   *Audience:* ______________________________

   *Subtopics:* ______________________________

   ______________________________

   ______________________________

   ______________________________

   ______________________________

   ______________________________

   *Specific supports:* ______________________________

   ______________________________

   ______________________________

   ______________________________

   ______________________________

   ______________________________

   *Outline*

5. You have been asked by your psychology instructor to observe the behavior of people in closed, small spaces. You decide that elevators are ideal spaces for your observations. Record your specific observations of both verbal and nonverbal behaviors in the elevators of a local hotel and department store. Then write the paper summary for your instructor.

   *Purpose:* ______________________________

   *Audience:* ______________________________

   *Observations:* ______________________________

   ______________________________
   ______________________________
   ______________________________
   ______________________________
   ______________________________
   ______________________________
   ______________________________
   ______________________________
   ______________________________
   ______________________________

   *Outline*

# 4 Description

> *Describing a Porsche is far easier than describing democracy. Fortunately, most practical writing descriptions are of concrete objects. Describe* your *main mode of transportation.*

The key to writing a good description is attention to detail. Use specific words capable of creating a physical image in the mind of your reader. Avoid vague, general words, which do not. Some paragraphs will be written purely for a descriptive purpose, such as a job description, a product description, or a process description. However, most descriptions of objects, people, events, or ideas appear in paragraphs whose purpose is other than the descriptions themselves. For example, you may write a report recommending a copying machine purchase containing a description of the Xerox copier. The purpose of the report is to recommend. You use description to support your recommendation.

**Principles of Description**

The same principles apply to all descriptions. You should:

1. Use concrete words that create a vivid image in your reader's mind.
2. Use examples, statistics, or credible (believable) sources and authorities to support your description.
3. Assume your audience does not know much about your topic to avoid leaving out important details.

Categories of features of the object, person, event, or idea you are describing usually become subtopics in the paragraph. The features are often specific supports. For example, to describe an indoor soccer shoe to an uninformed audience would require a list of the shoe features in language the reader will understand: similarity to the style of a common tennis shoe; leather; no cleats, but tough rubber sole; ankle height; 12 eyelets for laces, etc. Sorted into categories, these features might be grouped in two categories: upper portion of shoe and lower portion of shoe. You may group features according to appearance and function or appearance, function, and price. Depending on the purpose of your paragraph and the intended audience, the number of categories and features will vary.

Description requires thinking skills applied to many kinds of writing. To accurately depict (show) an object, person, event, or idea, you might want to use a comparison ("An indoor soccer shoe looks like a black tennis shoe") or a definition ("An indoor soccer shoe belongs to the family of athletic footwear") to help readers actually "see" the shoe in their minds' eye. Description, too, is used in other kinds of writing. To compare and contrast, define, or analyze a process requires complete descriptions of your subject.

Describing abstract ideas presents the greatest challenge to beginning writers. How do you avoid using general, abstract language when you're describing something that can't be touched or seen? You must use words that are as concrete as possible. What evidence of your abstract idea exists in the material world? If you are describing the idea of inflation, for example, you might first place the term in its "class" or category of idea: "Inflation is an economic condition." Then you might describe specific characteristics of inflation: "Inflation is shown in price increases for real, physical goods. A gallon of milk cost 56¢ in 1968 and now costs about $2." Show the idea "inflation" in terms your audience will understand.

Improve the quality of your descriptions by choosing specific words. As your vocabulary grows, you will use an increasing number of concrete, exact, precise words to communicate your meaning. Instead of *good, a lot, nice, many, something, this,* and *it,* substitute meaningful words that transmit a picture to the reader. *A lot of people* might be better stated as *35 percent of our undergraduates* for improved specificity. Review all your sentences word by word to weed out and replace general or vague words.

### Outline for a Description

The *topic sentence* states your purpose. The reader should know without reading further than the first sentence what you will be describing and perhaps even why you are describing it. The subtopics, or roman numerals of the outline, should name the general category or class of features. The features, or characteristics of the object of your description, should become specific supports: the As, Bs, and Cs. Specific supports must be written in concrete, exact language. Your outline should be organized in parallel fashion, as all others have been, and move from the least specific to most specific detail. Here is a brainstormed list of characteristics one student developed for an outline and paragraph:

*Purpose:* To describe an idea for a holiday window scene in a major department store.

*Ideas:* Santa and Mrs. Claus in rocking chairs, potbelly stove, elves bringing in toys on small sleds, Rudolph the Reindeer looking on, snow and "barber pole" for North Pole. Featured toys: science kits, cars and trucks, radios, electric train. Featured clothes: on elves, boys' sizes 4–6x; in Mrs. Claus's lap, junior girls' sizes Angora line. Much snow, hanging snowflakes, movable train, and elves. Music possible.

*Topic sentence:* Here is my idea for the State Street window dressing to appear November 15–January 3.

**I.** Theme: Toyland, North Pole
- A. Characters: Santa, Mrs. Claus, elves, Rudolph
- B. Setting: North Pole, snow and ice, cozy kitchen, and perhaps music ("Toyland")
- C. Action: elves bringing toys, eating cookies, watching train; movable figures

**II.** Merchandise featured
- A. Boys' clothing: shirts and corduroy pants
- B. Girls' clothing: angora sweaters
- C. Toys: science kits, trains, radios, cars, and trucks

*Paragraph*

Here is a description of the Christmas State Street window display to appear between November 15 and January 3. The theme of Toyland will appeal to passersby with children. Santa and Mrs. Claus, seated in kitchen rockers before a potbelly stove, look upon elves bringing in toys for inspection. Rudolph the Reindeer watches from the right foreground corner. All characters have rotating heads and movable joints. Snow and ice, both from RealDisplay, Inc., and a moving train contribute to the enchanting scene. Merchandise best displayed in this window will appeal to children. Tonka toys and trucks, bright red and green, microscope and chemistry sets, and the Lionel train already mentioned, should be in the window foreground on elves' sleds. Smart Radios, near the rockers, will coordinate well with angora sweaters in primary colors. The elves' clothing, by KidWorks, should provide amusing contrast.

Notice how this writer became even more specific while writing out the paragraph. "Science kits" became "microscope and chemistry sets." The positions of the characters are stated more precisely. This paragraph could, of course, provide even greater detail. Point out specifically how the paragraph might be improved.

### Spatial Relationships

*Spatial* refers to the placement of real objects in space. When you give directions to someone lost in your city, you use your ability to describe movement in terms of directions, reference points, and distance. Analyzing and then describing locations, buildings, rooms, and other spaces requires frequent use of prepositional phrases. Here are some common prepositions useful in writing descriptions:

| | | | | |
|---|---|---|---|---|
| in | of | by | under | around |
| at | on | to | beneath | above |

Expressions of direction, placement, or location are also useful:

on the right (left) of
adjacent (next) to
parallel to
perpendicular to
at a right angle
turn 180° (1/2 of a complete circle)
north, east, south, west, northeast, northwest, southeast, southwest
directly
beside

An important consideration when writing a description based on spatial relationships is to describe objects in some order. For example, in describing a room, you may begin at the left wall and proceed in order of objects in the room to the right wall. Or you may divide space into foreground and background, or use the hours on the face of a clock as reference points.

**Summary**

Descriptions are most likely to be written in response to a request from either an instructor or employer. Close observation, attention to detail, and use of specific, concrete language are three important skills to develop. When these skills are employed, they allow the reader to "see" what is being described. Whether descriptions are embedded in other kinds of writing or standing alone, organizing the description according to the relationship of things in space is a useful technique for achieving clarity.

## DESCRIPTION SCORE SHEET

5=Excellent    4=Good    3=Average    2=Weak    1=Poor    0=Failure

| | |
|---|---|
| *Content* | |
| Quality of ideas (interesting, amusing, original) | 5 4 3 2 1 0 |
| Development of ideas (details, examples) beyond a simple list | 5 4 3 2 1 0 |
| Sufficient specific ideas or examples | 5 4 3 2 1 0 |
| *Structure* | |
| Topic sentence: | |
| Appears first in paragraph. | 5 4 3 2 1 0 |
| Refines broad topic. | 5 4 3 2 1 0 |
| Expresses main idea of paragraph. | 5 4 3 2 1 0 |
| Ideas in body of the paragraph relate to the topic sentence. | 5 4 3 2 1 0 |
| *Readability* | |
| Transitions appear where necessary between ideas. | 5 4 3 2 1 0 |
| Grammar | 5 4 3 2 1 0 |
| Word choice | 5 4 3 2 1 0 |
| Punctuation | 5 4 3 2 1 0 |
| Spelling | 5 4 3 2 1 0 |

## EXERCISES

1. Write one-paragraph descriptions of the following topics. You may change or refine the topics to focus on a subject you are familiar with.

   A new product your company has just developed or purchased for its own use

   An architectural style you've identified on your campus or in the city you live in

Your experience with a company's faulty electronic product—a radio or tape player, for example—and ask for an adjustment (a letter of complaint)

A rare fishing lure that you want to order from a specialty tackle dealer

The conditions of the warranty, in response to a customer's complaint about a malfunctioning piece of farm equipment

An ideal vacation location to a friend interested in meeting new people

A job description for each of the following minimum wage positions: food server, sales clerk, pizza delivery person, movie usher

The effects of alcohol consumption on muscle reflex responses

An advertisement describing a condominium

The behavior of a gorilla or other primate at the zoo

The behavior of a blind date

A cat approaching a bird

The express lane in a supermarket

Your family's celebration of a favorite holiday

2. Write a one-paragraph description of the following abstract ideas for an uninformed audience.

   Interest rate

   Mileage

   Computer programming

Radio astronomy

Direct mail marketing

Serology

Mortgage

Rent

Nutrition

Life insurance

Insulation

Profit

Wealth

Efficiency

3. Using a map of your campus, describe the location of the following buildings to a new student. You might begin with a description of the campus location within the city, using city street names.

   Student center

Book store

Library

Gymnasium

4. Describe your plan to redecorate a room of your house, apartment, or dormitory living space. Draw the room, indicate the placement of major furniture pieces, and note the location of windows, doors, and other permanent features. Then write your descriptive paragraph, using the drawing as a guide.

5. Plan your annual spring planting of garden space. Describe the dimensions of the garden, spacing of rows, types of seeds and seedlings you intend to plant, and the way you expect your garden to appear in midsummer. Your audience for this description is unfamiliar with gardening.

6. A realtor has asked you to describe your home to potential buyers in a short descriptive paragraph published by the city's board of realtors. A photograph of your home will accompany the description. Target a potential market for your home—young couples without children, retired couples, large families, single professionals—before writing your description. Include only main features that will appeal to your targeted market and information that is essential to all home buyers.

# 5 The Longer Message

> *Whether assigned by your boss or instructor, the longer message needn't overwhelm you. "Chunk" it into smaller, manageable parts and tackle them one at a time.*

The same rules of organization apply to multiparagraph messages as to single-paragraph messages. They are used on a larger scale in longer messages. For example, writing a clear topic sentence for a paragraph translates to writing a clear thesis sentence for a report.

## Structure of the Longer Message

The following illustration shows the relationship of the single-paragraph message to a multiparagraph message in its most basic form:

| *Paragraph* | | *Longer Message* |
|---|---|---|
| Topic sentence (Main idea) | ———> | Thesis statement (Main idea) |
| Subtopic sentences within the paragraph | ———> | Topic sentences of separate paragraphs |
| Support sentences in body of single paragraph | ———> | Integrated into paragraphs of longer message |

An outline for either a paragraph or a longer message will look very similar, especially in main headings. An outline for a longer message will have more subheadings, representing additional details. The outline that follows may serve to structure a paragraph or a longer message.

*Topic sentence/Thesis sentence:* Managers conducting international business must study and practice intercultural business communication skills.

**I.** Communicating with people in different cultures requires an understanding of one's own culture.

**II.** Understanding the culture of the host country is an essential component of effective intercultural business communication.

**III.** Learning and practicing writing skills that contribute to effective communication will facilitate intercultural communication.

Now read the paragraph that was developed from this outline to see how the paragraph contains the structure of the longer message.

| *Topic sentence:* | = | *Thesis statement:* |
|---|---|---|
| Managers conducting international business must study and practice intercultural business communication skills. | <— | Thesis statement is the same as the topic sentence. |
| *First subtopic sentence:* | <— | First topic sentence is the same as the first subtopic. |

| | | |
|---|---|---|
| Communicating with people in different cultures first requires understanding one's own. | | |
| *Explanation / facts / examples:* | <— | Same |
| For example, North Americans should understand how individualism influences business practices in their culture. | | Additional explanation<br>Additional facts<br>Additional examples<br>Expanded examples |
| *Second subtopic sentence:* | <— | Second topic sentence is the same as the second subtopic. |
| Understanding the culture of the host country is also an essential component of effective intercultural communication. | | |
| *Explanation / facts / examples:* | <— | Same |
| While individualism is an obvious trait of North American culture, concern for the group and community exists in marked contrast in Japanese culture. | | Additional explanation<br>Additional facts<br>Additional examples<br>Expanded examples |
| *Third subtopic sentence:* | <— | Third topic sentence is the same as the third subtopic. |
| Finally, learning and practicing writing skills that contribute to effective communicating will facilitate intercultural communication. | | |

| | | |
|---|---|---|
| *Explanation / facts / examples:* | <— | Same |
| Messages constructed for routine business correspondence in Japan, for example, would be most successful using an indirect approach. | | Additional explanation<br>Additional facts<br>Additional examples<br>Expanded examples |

## Aids to the Reader

The longer message demands that readers spend more time and concentrate harder. To help readers understand the message easily in the first reading, the writer provides several aids:

- An introductory paragraph that may include, in addition to the thesis statement:
  - An opening statement
  - A paper preview
- Headings in the body of the message
- A concluding paragraph

### Opening the Introductory Paragraph

You have begun the paragraphs you have written so far with the topic sentence. You *may* begin longer messages with a thesis sentence. However, it is customary in longer messages to put the thesis sentence in an introductory paragraph that begins with an opening statement that may be one, two, or more sentences long.

This opening statement serves an important purpose. It helps to orient readers to the topic and prepares them for the main idea introduced in the thesis statement. The length of the introductory statement depends on your assessment of the reader:

- *Are the readers knowledgeable about this topic?* If your answer is "yes," then you can use a short opening statement. If your answer is "no" or "I don't know," then you must give more information in your opening.
- *Are the readers interested in this topic?* If your answer is "yes," then, again, a short opening statement will do. If your answer is "no" or "I don't know," then you may have to consider techniques to interest them.

Writers use several techniques to begin messages. Selection of the technique to use in your message depends on your answers to the previous questions as well as on the tone (the way you wish the reader to perceive your message) you wish to establish. Read through the list of techniques for opening messages to decide which would work best for the message about North American/Japanese business communication.

1. *Historical background:* This can be a brief discussion of events or ideas that came before the situation that your message addresses.

   *Example:* For decades after World War II, Americans dominated world trade, and manufacturing businesses were primarily located in North America. Then Japanese and American businesses began to establish a solid trading relationship. The importance of communicating in the global marketplace increased.

2. *Question:* A well phrased question about the subject catches readers' interest and encourages further reading to see how the writer is going to answer.

   *Example:* If you were asked how best to communicate with a Japanese business person, what would you say?

3. *Quotation:* A short quotation, especially if it is by somebody whom the reader will recognize and who is closely related to the topic, will attract the reader's attention.

   *Example:* "There are truths on this side of the Pyrénées which are falsehoods on the other."—Blaise Pascal, *Pensées.*

4. *Factual information:* A fact or statistic from a believable source, such as an official spokesperson or newspaper, will lend authority to your message.

   *Example:* American auto executives have learned the value of slower paced business meetings with their Japanese partners. The CEO of Toyota in America states, "Consensus takes time and our long meetings provide that opportunity."

### Previewing the Message

In addition to the opening statement and the thesis, the introductory paragraph has a third element that helps the reader: the message preview. This preview acts much as a map for a driver or a blueprint for an architect. It lets the reader know the main divisions of the paper and, in doing so, informs the reader of the topics the writer will discuss.

Where does the preview come from? The preview comes from ideas expressed in the roman numeral items in the outline. If we go back to the outline first developed for the sample paper, you see that the three main ideas about intercultural communication are:

**I.** Learn one's own culture.
**II.** Learn the host culture.
**III.** Practice writing for an international audience.

These, then, are the ideas that will form the preview of the message. Putting the opening statement, the thesis, and the preview together will produce this introductory paragraph.

> For decades after World War II, Americans dominated world trade, and factories were primarily located in North America. When Japanese and American manufacturers began to establish a solid trading relationship, the importance of communicating in the global marketplace increased. Managers conducting international business must study and practice intercultural business communication skills. These skills include understanding one's own culture, learning the host culture, and practicing writing skills for an international audience.

### Body of the Message

When you have finished the introductory paragraph, you are ready to begin the body of the paper. It will follow the pattern of organization you set up in the preview. You must write at least one paragraph about each of the topics mentioned in the preview *in the order* established in the preview. The main idea of the first topic sentence you write in the body of the message would be about the importance of understanding one's own culture; the second topic sentence would be about learning other cultures; the third, about practicing communication skills. The important thing to remember is that each paragraph has a topic sentence, and each topic sentence relates to the thesis sentence. (You could, of course, write more than one paragraph on these topics if you had sufficient information to do so, but for now we will assume one paragraph for each topic.)

### Headings

You can improve the readability of the body of the message by using informative headings to separate its main parts. Informative headings tell the reader what each part of the message is about and function similarly to headlines in a newspaper. Using a simple system of headings, you will have as many headings as you have items in the preview and, indeed, the content of the headings will be the same as the content of items in the preview. Thus, if the preview of the sample paper is, "These skills include understanding one's own culture, learning the host culture, and practicing writing skills for an international audience," the headings would also contain these ideas.

Headings are words or, more often, phrases that come before each new part of the paper. Very long reports may use four or five levels of headings. We will use only one level and place these headings on their own line at the left margin. To make the headings stand out from the rest of the message, they will be underlined. On the next page is an example that illustrates placement of headings.

SAMPLE REPORT WITH HEADINGS

**The Importance of Intercultural Communication Skills for Managers**

For decades after World War II, Americans dominated world trade, and factories were primarily located in North America. When Japanese and American manufacturers began to establish a solid trading relationship, the importance of communicating in the global marketplace increased. Managers conducting international business must study and practice intercultural business communication skills. These skills include understanding one's own culture, learning the host culture, and practicing writing skills for an international audience.

Understanding One's Own Culture

Communicating with people in different cultures first requires an understanding of one's own culture. For example, North Americans should understand how individualism influences business practices in their culture. Rewards are made to individuals for achievement, and individuals are expected to make their good work highly visible. For example, sales representatives might be expected to report an extraordinarily high volume of sales to their superiors, highlighting their achievement in a memo.

Learning the Host Country's Culture

Learning the culture of the host country is also an essential component of effective intercultural communication. While individualism is an obvious trait of North American culture, concern for the group and community exists in marked contrast in Japanese culture. Individuals do not draw attention to their singular successes in the Japanese organization. They would be uncomfortable in meetings that focused on individual achievement. Instead, employees would point to the combined efforts of their team in accomplishing an organizational goal.

Practicing Writing Skills for Intercultural Communication

Finally, learning and practicing writing skills that contribute to effective communication will facilitate intercultural communication. Messages constructed for routine business correspondence in Japan, for example, would be most successful using an indirect format. Business letters in Japan often start with a reference to the weather and then make polite inquiries about the reader's health before getting to the main point. The North American audience prefers a direct organizational pattern. Letters often begin with the main point of business. If they include any personal references at all, these come at the end of the message. Both patterns reflect something about the cultures. The sensitive writer will appreciate the differences to improve the effectiveness of communications.

Here are a few points to keep in mind about headings:

1. Headings are in parallel grammatical form.
2. Headings do not end with a period (although if they are put in question form they should end with a question mark).
3. An *informative* heading does not precede the concluding paragraph. Some writers will use the *descriptive* heading Conclusion before the concluding paragraph, however.
4. Do not leave a heading as the last line on the page.

### The Concluding Paragraph

The concluding paragraph is not part of your formal outline. Some messages don't have conclusions at all. When a concluding paragraph is called for, its purpose is usually to summarize what the writer has said. Concluding paragraphs are useful particularly in long messages where they refresh the reader's memory concerning the writer's main points and reinforce the writer's ideas. Thus, the concluding paragraph should mention the thesis and main points of the message. It may also refer to the opening statement to give the reader a sense of closure in that the writer has come full circle and ended on the opening thought.

Here is a concluding paragraph for the sample paper.

> As American business people reach out to find new markets for their products, they find a need to cultivate new communications skills. They must first bring their own characteristics to a level of conscious understanding. They must also

learn how these characteristics compare and contrast with characteristics of potential trading partners. Then they must put this knowledge into practice when communicating in writing with business people outside the United States. By themselves, these steps may not guarantee business success. However, they are a necessary first step in understanding and building relationships.

Reminders to help you prepare concluding paragraphs:

1. Instead of copying your opening paragraph word for word, restate it.
2. Don't introduce new information in your concluding paragraph.
3. Keep your nerve. The concluding paragraph should not reveal a change of mind about what you've said in the body of the paper or a change in the tone of your paper.

## Summary

The longer message is in many ways an expansion of the structural elements of the paragraph. The longer message may give background in the opening paragraph to prepare readers for the thesis statement. Other features are added to the longer message to help readers keep their place or find their place if they are distracted while reading. These are the paper preview and headings in the body of the message that reflect the parts announced in the preview. A final feature of the longer message is often a concluding paragraph that summarizes the writer's ideas.

## LONGER MESSAGE SCORE SHEET

5=Excellent 4=Good 3=Average 2=Weak 1=Poor 0=Failure

| | |
|---|---|
| *Content* | |
| Quality of ideas (interesting, amusing, original) | 5 4 3 2 1 0 |
| Development of ideas (details, examples) | 5 4 3 2 1 0 |
| Sufficient specific ideas | 5 4 3 2 1 0 |
| Interest to reader | 5 4 3 2 1 0 |
| *Structure* | |
| Begins with opening statement that attracts the reader's attention. | 5 4 3 2 1 0 |
| Contains a thesis statement that: | |
| Is linked logically to the introductory statement. | 5 4 3 2 1 0 |
| Expresses the main idea of the message. | 5 4 3 2 1 0 |
| Contains a preview of the main ideas of the message. | 5 4 3 2 1 0 |
| The preview is written as a separate sentence. | 5 4 3 2 1 0 |
| The preview has at least three main points about the thesis. | 5 4 3 2 1 0 |
| The topic sentences appear first in each paragraph. | 5 4 3 2 1 0 |
| Each topic sentence develops a point given in the preview. | 5 4 3 2 1 0 |
| Topic sentences follow the order given in the preview. | 5 4 3 2 1 0 |
| Ideas in the body of paragraphs relate to the topic sentence (unity). | 5 4 3 2 1 0 |
| *Readability* | |
| Transitions appear where necessary between ideas. | 5 4 3 2 1 0 |
| Headings | |
| Are appropriately formatted. | 5 4 3 2 1 0 |
| Follow the order of ideas of the preview. | 5 4 3 2 1 0 |
| Grammar | 5 4 3 2 1 0 |
| Word choice | 5 4 3 2 1 0 |
| Punctuation | 5 4 3 2 1 0 |
| Spelling | 5 4 3 2 1 0 |

## EXERCISES

1. Read the *first paragraphs* of five magazine articles. What techniques do the the authors use to open their first paragraphs? Explain which one caught your interest best and why.

   *Techniques*

   a. ______

   b. ______

   c. ______

   d. ______

   e. ______

   *Best*

   ______

2. Read the *concluding paragraphs* of five magazine articles. What other techniques besides the one described here do the authors use? Would these techniques be acceptable in business writing? Explain your answer.

*Techniques*

a. ______________________________

______________________________

______________________________

______________________________

b. ______________________________

______________________________

______________________________

______________________________

c. ______________________________

______________________________

______________________________

______________________________

d. ______________________________

______________________________

______________________________

______________________________

e. ______________________________

______________________________

______________________________

______________________________

*Acceptable*

______________________________

______________________________

______________________________

______________________________

3. Show the relationship between the following one-paragraph message and a longer message by showing which parts of this paragraph would make a thesis sentence and topic sentences for paragraphs. Use the sentence numbers to identify the thesis and topic sentences. Then write a preview sentence.

   [1]Michigan's Upper Peninsula abounds in regional food products. [2]Pasties are meat-filled pastries, imported by Scandinavian immigrants. [3]Popular pasty stands line the highways along Lake Superior. [4]Vegetarian pasties cater to the "downstate" travelers' tastes. [5]Fruit trees provide ample produce for making jelly, jam, wine, and preserves. [6]These trees include the sugarplum, chokecherry, and wild apple. [7]Wild berries are also in ample supply. [8]Strawberries—some as big as your thumb—begin to ripen in early July. [9]Then come blueberries, raspberries, blackberries, and thimbleberries. [10]All of these gourmet products are available to the tourists who want to sample regional foods.

   *Thesis sentence:* ____________________

   *Topic sentences:* ____________________

   *Preview sentence:* ______________________________

   ________________________________________

   ________________________________________

   ________________________________________

4. Read through the following groups of headings carefully. Which headings are not in parallel form? Rewrite headings so that they conform to parallel structure.

   *Topic:* Survey of Viewers of WKZL-TV

   Age of Viewers ________________

   Sex of Viewers ________________

   Viewers' Favorite Programs ________________

   Musical Preferences ________________

   *Topic:* Training Library Volunteers

   How Can We Improve Knowledge? ________________

   Increasing Commitment ________________

   Improved Supervision ________________

   *Topic:* Exercise

   Is Exercise Necessary for Fitness? ________________

   Features of a Good Exercise Program ________________

   Should We Sponsor Employee Memberships at YMCA? ________________

   What Would a Company Fitness Center Cost? ________________

   *Topic:* Plans for the Annual Convention

   Hotel Visitation ________________

   Reserve Rooms ________________

   Schedule Speakers ________________

   Invite Members to Register ________________

5. Read the following outlines carefully. Write the introductory

paragraphs for these reports. Include an opening statement, a thesis statement, and a paper preview for each of them.

*Topic:* Attractions of the Southeastern United States

**I.** Availability of jobs
  A. Growth in manufacturing
  B. Opportunities in medicine

**II.** Low cost of living
  A. Cost of housing
  B. Cost of fuel
  C. Cost of food

*Topic:* Employee Benefits at Ludwig Industries

**I.** Insurance program
   A. Hospitalization
   B. Major medical
   C. Life insurance
   D. Disability insurance

**II.** Paid holidays
   A. National holidays
   B. Annual vacation

**III.** Retirement program

A. Company pension plan
B. Employee annuity plan
C. Stock purchase plan

## CASES

For these cases, use the space provided in the book and/or additional sheets as necessary.

1. Review the topics in Exercise 1, Chapter 4. Select one topic. Develop the topic into a longer message that has an introductory paragraph (opening statement, thesis, preview), at least three paragraphs in the body of the paper with headings, and a concluding paragraph.

2. Your best friend has named you as a reference for a position with the State Volunteer Corps. Corps members work with economically disadvantaged youth in urban and rural areas of your state. The position includes engaging the youth in meaningful activities, building their self-esteem, introducing them to job skills, and interesting them in higher education opportunities.

   Write a letter of recommendation for your friend to Harold Willis, Director of Human Resources, State Volunteer Corps, in the capital city of your state. Use the structure for longer messages.

3. You are a member of the 2001 Committee in your town. Each committee member joins a writing subcommittee of the 2001 Report Task Force to compose a section of the 2001 Report. You are reporting on one area of town life. The areas that you may choose to work on are:

   Economics

   Health and Human Services

   Parks and Recreation

   Governmental Affairs

   The 2001 Committee has chosen a common format for all parts of the report. Thus, no matter what subcommittee you've chosen to work on, you will report on:

   What the situation is now regarding the topic you have chosen.

   What changes you would like to see made and how those changes would benefit the community.

   What the town must do to implement the changes you describe.

4. Having recently purchased a home computer for personal use, you have decided to investigate spreadsheet software to use in home budgeting. You are a beginning user with little money to spend on an expensive, complex software package. You have outlined major expense and income categories, and would like to find a package that meets your criteria.

   Draft a letter to Software International requesting information about HomeBudget, software that you saw advertised in a personal computing magazine. Be sure to include information about yourself, your computer, and your needs.

5. As a student in a communication class, you have been assigned to write a one-page information sheet for international students at your university describing a college tradition. Special events, college ceremonies or rituals, and college holidays are unknown to international students who would like to read your descriptions of these special traditions.

   Write the one-page information sheet describing a tradition in simple paragraph format for inclusion in a larger notebook collection of essays.

6. The president of your Campus Student Organization has requested a report describing the various student groups on campus. The report, a two- or three-page handout to be distributed in a freshman orientation program, should summarize the purpose, membership, and activities of all recognized student groups on your campus.

   Prepare the short report in a format your audience will find easy to read and can keep as a reference.

7. You must select a local radio station to carry the advertisements for your athletic store. Listen to the programming of all local radio stations in your area and determine the best station, time of day, and days for your 15-second ads.

   Begin by defining the audience (target market) you wish to reach. Then prepare a report for your store manager, recommending your choice. Include the data you have collected in a format you believe your manager will expect. See the sample report in this chapter for ideas about page layout, headings, and spacing.

# 6 Process Description

*Have you ever tried to program a VCR or put together furniture ("Some assembly required!") using hard-to-follow instructions? Writing process descriptions clearly can be challenging. Think about instructions as "recipes" that a reader must understand.*

*Process description* is a common message pattern that you may be asked to write while at work. Writing a set of instructions, explaining how you performed a task, and describing how something works are typical process descriptions.

Process descriptions require close attention to detail and the order of events. Time is an important element to consider in writing the message. Recall a simple set of instructions that you have followed in the past week. Perhaps you filled your own gas tank at a self-service pump. If you needed to explain the process to someone totally unfamiliar with self-service gas pumps, what important steps should you explain? You must consider details that you might not ordinarily think about when explaining a process to an uninformed audience. And attention to the order of events in the process is critical to the individual's success in performing the described task.

## Writing the Process Description

Two critical thinking skills essential in writing process descriptions are an ability to order steps in a process and an ability to predict how a reader will respond to your words. To write a process description, follow these steps:

1. List the probable steps in the process.
2. Organize the list by putting the steps in a logical order.
3. Determine whether each step in the list would be easily understood by an uninformed audience.
4. Revise the list so that each step is completely understandable.

Process descriptions may seem simple when you first think about them. However, as you have probably already discovered, writing in precise detail for an uninformed audience requires effort. To show you how a simple process description is written, study this example of steps in "figuring a percentage":

1. Determine the number value that represents the whole.
2. Key in the number for which you need to find a "percent" value on a calculator.
3. Key in the whole number value determined in step 1.
4. Press the division key.

In a simple process like this, you may still need to add an example or give an illustration to aid in reader understanding. Also note that each step in the process begins with an active command verb: "Determine," "Key," "Key," and "Press." Instructions should be written this way so that the reader is told what to do in a command voice. Each step is also numbered and contains only one idea. Reading separate, numbered items helps the reader understand the order of events.

To formalize a process description, you should also include an introduction explaining the purpose of the process, a list of materials the reader may need to perform the process, and illustrations and hints as necessary. Here is a more formal version of a process description to instruct an uninformed audience.

How to Refinish an Oak Table

An old oak dinner table found at an auction can become a good-looking piece of furniture. With the following materials and about three hours of your time, you will transform the piece into an object of beauty.

Materials needed:

1 quart varnish and paint remover

2 standard three-inch paint brushes

Steel wool

A dozen cotton rags

2-inch paint scraper

An old toothbrush

1 quart polyurethane clear finish

Procedure:

1. Choose a well ventilated work area.
2. Cover the floor of the work area with a drop cloth or newspaper.
3. Place the table in the center of the work area.
4. Apply a generous coat of varnish and paint remover to the table surfaces according to the instructions on the can.
5. Remove all old paint and varnish from table surfaces using the scraper, steel wool, and toothbrush.

   Repeat step 5 as often as necessary to accomplish the complete removal of old paint and varnish.
6. Apply one or two coats of clear polyurethane finish to the clean table surfaces.

*Hint:* To protect your hands during this process, wear plastic gloves and rinse your hands frequently.

Some process descriptions, such as explanations of a process you have already performed or plan to perform, may be written in paragraph form. Your supervisor, for example, may request an explanation of a new procedure you have implemented to route office mail. A short memo written in paragraph form would be appropriate. Perhaps your instructor has requested a description of the methods you used to research a problem. In this case, you would include a "Methods" or "Procedures" paragraph in the paper or report you have prepared. The critical thinking skills involved in process descriptions remain the same: You must order the sequence of events logically and pay close attention to detail. You must not assume that readers can fill in missing steps for themselves or read between the lines. Explain each step in the process, no matter how obvious the step seems to you.

Here is a paragraph that explains the steps involved in loading a floppy disk into the Atari computer's disk drive system. Note that a clear topic sentence is followed by steps, or subtopics, and specific examples in parallel design.

> To load a floppy disk into the Atari 810 disk drive, which accompanies the Atari 800 computer, follow these four simple steps. First, hold the floppy disk so that the notched end of the disk can be inserted forward into the drive's slotted opening. The label will be on top of the disk and closest to you. Second, gently push the disk forward through the slotted opening until you feel the disk engage with a "click" sound. You will hear the low hum of the machine come to a halt. Third, secure the disk by flipping the lever down over the opening. Only one lever appears on the drive front, making this step foolproof. Fourth, press the power button to "boot," or activate, the disk.

### Illustrating a Process Description

One picture may be worth a thousand words in process description. If you have ever bought a product that you have had to assemble yourself, you know that the manufacturer has included an illustration (and sometimes several illustrations) to accompany the directions. The same is true even of products that are simple to operate.

To use an illustration, often a line drawing or photograph, in a process description, follow these rules.

1. Number the illustration: for example, Figure 1.
2. Give your illustration a title: for example, Figure 1. Espresso coffee machine.
3. Label the parts of your illustration.
4. Place your labels as close as you can to the illustrated part to avoid confusing readers.
5. Refer to the illustration in your written process description: for example, See Figure 1.

Study Figure 1 to see how to use these directions.

**Figure 1.** Espresso coffee machine.

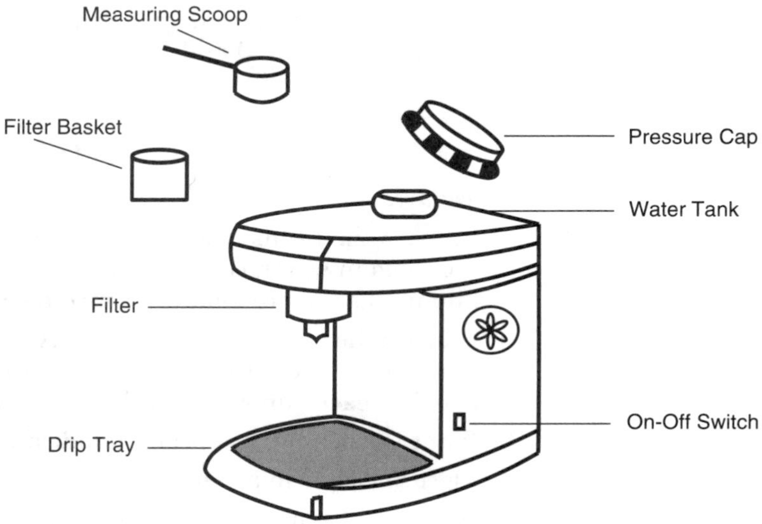


## Writing a Lab Report

Another kind of process description is a lab report. A student enrolled in an introductory physics course prepared this lab report. Note the standard lab report sections: Purpose, Materials, Procedure, Data, and Conclusion.

Lab #1
Physics 100
Tom Supnick
January 12, 19XX

**Plant Growth and Seed Positioning**

*Purpose:* To determine whether the position of a planted bean seed affects the growth of a plant.

*Materials:*

4 paper cups
1 cup vermiculite
Water
50-milliliter graduated cylinder
4 beans, similarly shaped, and each weighing between .9 and 1.25 grams
Lighted area
Scale
Ruler
Permanent marker
Tape
Shallow aluminum pan

*Procedure:*

1. Prepare the beans one day before the experiment by soaking them in water, covering the beans completely, in an aluminum dish approximately 1 inch deep.
2. Prepare the cups by labeling them A, B, C, and D and attach a picture to each that shows the position of the bean in the cup. Fill each cup with 2 inches of vermiculite.
3. Plant the bean in the position indicated on each cup.
4. Place the cups in a well-lit area.
5. Water the beans daily, making sure that each time you give each bean the same amount of water for that day.
6. Make observations for one week, noting the appearance of each planting.
7. After one week, dig up the beans (carefully, so as not to disturb the original position), and compare the results of each bean's growth. Then compare your results with your 25 classmates' results.

8. Record the data and observations.

*Data:*

| | Water Amount Given | Growth |
|---|---|---|
| Day 1 | 5 ml. | None |
| Day 2 | 5 ml. | None |
| Day 3 | 20 ml. | None |
| Day 4 | None | None |
| Day 5 | 2 ml. | Yes |
| Day 6 | 15 ml. | Yes |
| Day 7 | 15 ml. | Yes |

Day 8: The plants separated from the soil appeared as shown:

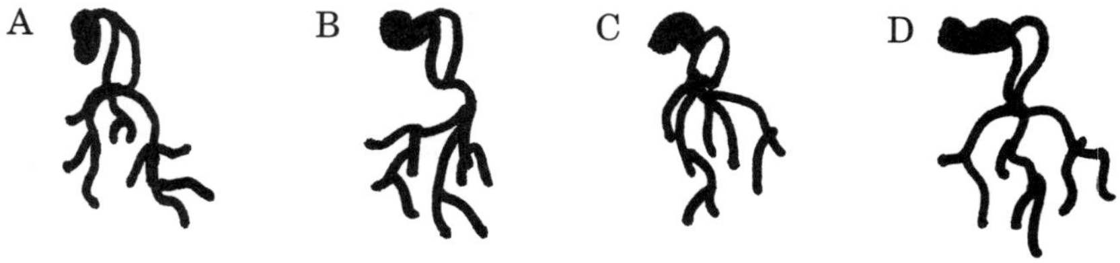


*Note:* Beans did not sprout until Day 5.

*Conclusion:* Based on these observations, bean growth does not appear to be affected by the position of the seed. Twenty-five classmates reached the same conclusion.

## Introductory Paragraph

## List of Materials

Procedures
(or Steps in Operation)

1. ______________________________

______________________________

2. ______________________________

______________________________

3. ______________________________

______________________________

4. ______________________________

______________________________

## Summary

Process descriptions enable you to give many different kinds of instructions. Yet all process descriptions have two requirements:

- Ability to analyze the needs of an audience;
- Ability to list every step in the process, to organize the list, and to test and revise the process description if needed.

While short process descriptions may be written in paragraph form, formatting (laying out text on a page to attract and direct the reader) is a key element in making longer process descriptions readable. After you explain the purpose of the process description, listing steps in the process helps the reader follow your instructions. Including a labeled illustration which you refer to when listing the steps also clarifies your instructions.

## PROCESS DESCRIPTION SCORE SHEET

5=Excellent 4=Good 3=Average 2=Weak 1=Poor 0=Failure

| | |
|---|---|
| *Content* | |
| Coverage of all information reader needs to complete the process. (*Note:* If paper doesn't fulfill this criterion, nothing else counts.) | 5 4 3 2 1 0 |
| Clarity of explanations (Any high school graduate should be able to follow the directions.) | 5 4 3 2 1 0 |
| Definition/explanation of abstract/technical terms | 5 4 3 2 1 0 |
| List of tools/materials needed to complete the process | 5 4 3 2 1 0 |
| Illustration of object when needed | 5 4 3 2 1 0 |
| Explanatory title for illustration | 5 4 3 2 1 0 |
| Labels for parts of the illustration | 5 4 3 2 1 0 |
| Interest to audience | 5 4 3 2 1 0 |
| *Structure* | |
| Thesis statement: | |
| Appears first in paragraph. | 5 4 3 2 1 0 |
| Refines broad topic. | 5 4 3 2 1 0 |
| Expresses main idea of the paragraph. | 5 4 3 2 1 0 |
| Body of paragraph: | |
| Follows order of use of object. | 5 4 3 2 1 0 |
| Gives one instruction at a time. | 5 4 3 2 1 0 |
| Phrases instructions as commands. | 5 4 3 2 1 0 |
| Gives "hints" or special instructions as necessary. | 5 4 3 2 1 0 |
| *Readability* | |
| Grammar | 5 4 3 2 1 0 |
| Word choice | 5 4 3 2 1 0 |
| Punctuation | 5 4 3 2 1 0 |
| Spelling | 5 4 3 2 1 0 |

## EXERCISES

1. Follow the method for writing a simple process description using these topics:

   *Inflating a bicycle tire*

   *Frying an egg*

*Sewing a button on a coat*

*Cleaning a stereo needle*

2. Write a process description in the format your instructor designates for one of the following processes.

   Changing a tire

   Balancing a checkbook

   Accessing a mainframe computer

   Constructing a bird feeder

   Changing the oil in a car

   Studying for an exam

   Researching a company before an interview

   Planning a wedding reception

   Giving a speech

   Writing a bill of sale

   Preparing a balance sheet

   Registering for classes

   Finding city hall in your city

   Doing laundry for the first time

   Waxing your skis

   Cleaning your rifle

   Planning your vacation

   Preparing your garden for planting

3. Prepare an illustration of a simple object that has at least five but no more than ten parts.

4. Vocabulary building:

   Clarity ______________________________

   Consistent ______________________________

   Designate ______________________________

   Distinct ______________________________

   Engage ______________________________

   Enhance ______________________________

   Essential ______________________________

   Formalize ______________________________

   Implement ______________________________

   Notched ______________________________

   Numerical ______________________________

   Predict ______________________________

   Probable ______________________________

   Revise ______________________________

   Sequence ______________________________

   Uninformed ______________________________

## CASES

1. *Organize a progress report.* Employees are often asked to write reports describing their progress on certain projects they've been assigned. These reports are organized by time. In this case study, you are asked to provide your supervisor with a written description of your progress on an assignment. Your position, job description, assignment, and report format are provided.

   *Position:* Telemarketing assistant for office supplies firm

   *Job description:* Assist marketing representative in charge of sales campaigns conducted by telephone for new and established accounts.

   *Assignment:* Telephone businesses and organizations that are potential customers for your new model of word processor with greater memory and increased office functions.

   *Progress:* You have contacted 30 businesses and organizations in your area who purchased the earlier model of the word processor being promoted. The phone campaign took three days to complete. Of the 30 contacts, 12 are interested in seeing the new model, 10 are definitely not in the market for a new model, and 8 wanted time to discuss the idea with staff. Your supervisor has asked for a detailed account of these calls in memo format.

   Use the following memo format.

   Date:

   To: Supervisor's name

   From: Your name

   Subject: Brief descriptive phrase of memo subject

   Begin the paragraph here. State your purpose in the first sentence. Do not indent sentences in this format. If you wish to use numbered statements corresponding to days, you may use single spacing within the statements and double space between them, as follows.

   1. Tuesday, September 1, etc.
   2. Wednesday, September 2, etc.

   When you have completed your paragraph, just stop. Memo format does not have a closing or signature. You may initial your name above, however.

Date: ____________________

To: ________________________________________

From: ________________________________________

Subject: ________________________________________

2. *Organize a trip report.* As a frequent traveler for your firm, you are required to prepare a report describing your trip expenses and itinerary. For this routine report, your company requests standard information: purpose of the trip, times and dates of the trip, location of meetings, lodging expenses and locations, meal expenses, and transportation expenses. A standard one-paragraph memo describing this information is sent along with receipts and charge slips. The memo is sent to the Director of Accounts Payable.

   Prepare reports for trips to San Antonio, Brooklyn (New York), and Phoenix. For each trip report, change the company name and purpose of your trip. Make up names for the companies visited, names of the hotels you stayed in, room rates, dates of your stay, transportation expenses, the dates and subjects of meetings.

Date: ____________________

To: ________________________________________

From: ________________________________________

Subject: ________________________________________

Date: ____________________

To: ________________________________________

From: ________________________________________

Subject: ________________________________________

Date: ____________________

To: ________________________________________

From: ________________________________________

Subject: ________________________________________

3. *Write computer documentation.* Electronic mail (e-mail) is a powerful tool that enables computer users to communicate with each other in local areas and around the world. Its use is growing in colleges and universities, businesses, and government organizations worldwide. E-mail has many advantages for the user, and nearly everyone enjoys using it. However, everyone who wants to use e-mail requires instructions.

   In this case study, you have just been hired by your college's computing center. Your first task is to write documentation (instructions for operating software) to enable first-time e-mail users on your campus to send a new message to another user on your campus.

   You may assume that each of these first-time users already has a computer account. Some of them are a little intimidated by computers, and others lack extensive knowledge of computers. Thus, they need step-by-step instructions. When you must use technical terms, be sure to explain them.

   Begin your instructions with logging onto e-mail. Use computer screens as illustrations as necessary to explain the process.

# 7 Compare and Contrast

*Which restaurant will you choose for a birthday dinner? Thinking about your choices involves the very same skills you use in writing a report based on comparison or contrast.*

*To compare* means to note similarities, or likenesses, in two or more objects, ideas, or people. Defined strictly, *to contrast* is to note differences rather than similarities. Most practical writing, though, which involves decision making or describing, requires a little of both. Writers do not have to limit their treatment of a subject to similarities or differences alone. Instead, comparisons are usually understood to include some contrasts as well.

Comparisons show an audience how you have analyzed two things, concepts, or individuals on a common basis. In school situations, comparisons are commonly called for on tests and other writing assignments: Compare this person to that person, this time in history with another, or this idea with that idea. The purpose of these comparisons is to clarify or illuminate the items for writer and reader alike. In professional situations, comparisons are most often used in making decisions and recommending choices to an audience. To resolve a problem in business or make a routine decision, you would compare options, or possible solutions to the problem. The rest of this chapter emphasizes the important use of making comparisons in practical, informational writing.

"Don't compare apples and oranges," a phrase you have probably heard, means that you must find a common element between the two things you're comparing even to consider comparing them. For example, comparing two models of refrigerators before deciding which one to purchase makes sense; comparing a goldfish to a shoe does not. Making your purpose for comparison clear to an audience is the first task a writer faces. Your reason for comparing two items can usually be stated in the topic sentence. Second, you must decide on what basis or bases (plural) you will compare the two objects. These points for comparison are called *criteria.* Once you have determined the reason for making a comparison, you are ready to begin forming criteria to make the comparison. Following the decision-making process provides you with both content and organization for your comparison paragraph(s).

Problem solving or decision making is also a thinking process. You make decisions every day, sometimes without being aware of them. For example, when deciding what kind of clothing to wear on a particular day, you probably consider where you'll be going, what kind of activity you must plan for, and whom you will be seeing during the day. Making a decision on the job involves this same process. Asking yourself questions about your day leads you to your decision about the most appropriate clothing. When you answer these questions, you have performed an important step in the decision-making, or problem-solving, process: establishing criteria that your solution (in this case, clothing) must meet. Not all problem solving involves explicit, or obvious, comparisons. However, most decisions require obvious comparisons. Tacit, or not obvious, comparisons will probably occur as well. In deciding what to wear, you may have compared items of clothing using the same criteria as guides to a solution.

**Thinking Process**

> *Problem to solve or decision to make:* What shall I wear today?
>
> *Criteria established for today:* The clothing must be warm, since the temperature is cold; the clothing should be informal, as I need only to attend class; the clothing must be comfortable, as I don't intend to change again.
>
> *Tacit comparisons:* Formal/informal clothing choices

If you were to attend a meeting that day and wanted to make a professional appearance, your criteria would be different. The first criterion might remain the same, but you would opt for less casual clothing that projected a different image to a different audience. You have compared clothing options and have made a decision based on criteria. Making decisions on the job or in school requires the same thinking process.

To compare and contrast ideas, people, or objects, then, you must have a basis or bases of comparison. These bases are the criteria. You can compare two automobiles using a set of criteria, as follows:

> *Problem / decision:* To buy a used car with the decision narrowed to two cars
>
> *Criteria:* It must cost under $4,000, get at least 25 miles per gallon, and be mechanically certified as needing no major repairs.

You are ready to compare the two cars using these three criteria.

Without first naming the criteria to use in making a comparison, you are in danger of making an invalid comparison. For example, if you listed different features for each of the two cars, arriving at a logical decision would be impossible. You wouldn't be able to say that one was better than another in any of the three categories. To compare, criteria are essential in both thinking through comparisons and writing out the comparison.

Think of some criteria for each of the following possible comparisons:

Cats/dogs as house pets
Personal computers
Two classes of the same required course
Two fashion designers' collections

In the first comparison, a purpose appears for you: Compare cats and dogs as *house pets.* The other comparisons, however, require you to develop a purpose for the comparison. For example, two personal computers can be compared, but a meaningful comparison requires a more limited purpose. Why are you comparing them? A comparison of an IBM and a Macintosh for a general-purpose home personal computer will demand different criteria than a comparison of the same two for a large business. A well defined topic—what you're comparing and why—is not only an excellent source for your thesis statement, it also makes establishing criteria for the comparison more accurate.

### Two Methods of Development

Once you have arrived at your topic and established the bases for comparison, the criteria, you are able to collect and sort information to use in the message. Comparison/contrast papers are perhaps the most logically organized of all patterns of development. The written organization parallels the thinking processes of decision making very closely. The thesis statement gives the purpose. The criteria you have developed correspond to topic sentences and form the preview for the paper. And the specific supports reflect your evaluation of information about the ideas, objects, or people being compared. This orderly pattern is the same for thinking, comparing, and writing.

Purpose for writing = Decision to be made and why =
Thesis statement

Criteria for comparing A and B =
Topic sentences and paper preview

Specific data or information about A and B =
Specific supports in paragraphs

Outlined, a comparison/contrast paragraph would appear like this:

**I.** Topic = Comparison of A and B for purpose X
- A. Criterion 1 = First basis of comparison
  1. How A meets this criterion; information on A
  2. How B meets this criterion; information on B
- B. Criterion 2 = Second basis of comparison
  1. How A meets this criterion; information on A
  2. How B meets this criterion; information on B

  ... and so on

A variation on this theme is simply to equate the two items being compared, A and B, with subtopic sentences and discuss how each meets the criteria in successive sentences, like this:

**I.** Purpose of comparing A and B = Topic sentence
- A. Object A
  1. Criterion 1: How A meets this criterion
  2. Criterion 2: How A meets this criterion
- B. Object B
  1. Criterion 1: How B meets this criterion
  2. Criterion 2: How B meets this criterion

For either method of organization, the criteria you use to compare the items *will be the same.* The information about the items will be different. For example, the criteria used to compare cars—price, mileage, and operating condition—must be the same bases of comparison for both cars. The specific supports, or information about each car, will be different and provide the body of your comparison. Both methods are appropriate for comparisons you must write about in school or on the job. If your comparison is lengthy, you may want to choose the second method. Readers may lose sight of your purpose if sentences see-saw from A to B. Determine the organization your audience would probably prefer.

To compare items A and B, use criteria 1, 2, and 3. State your purpose for comparing A and B, in addition to naming A and B, in the thesis statement.

*Diagram 1*

Thesis statement = Purpose

**I.** Item A
- A. Criterion 1
- B. Criterion 2
- C. Criterion 3

**II.** Item B
- A. Criterion 1
- B. Criterion 2
- C. Criterion 3

**or**

*Diagram 2*

Thesis statement = Purpose

**I.** Criterion 1
- A. Item A
- B. Item B

**II.** Criterion 2
- A. Item A
- B. Item B

**III.** Criterion 3
- A. Item A
- B. Item B

**Summary**

Comparing and contrasting two or more topics help writers clarify their thinking. Decisions are often based on comparisons and contrasts because these techniques highlight the relationship between ideas. To make a valid comparison or contrast, your topics first must have a common element. Then you must establish criteria for the comparison or contrast and organize your message using the topics and the criteria you have established for them.

## COMPARISON/CONTRAST SCORE SHEET

5=Excellent 4=Good 3=Average 2=Weak 1=Poor 0=Failure

| | |
|---|---|
| *Content* | |
| Opening statement attracts reader's attention. | 5 4 3 2 1 0 |
| Thesis statement states purpose for comparison/ contrast clearly. | 5 4 3 2 1 0 |
| Ideas (details, examples) are developed beyond a simple list. | 5 4 3 2 1 0 |
| Has sufficient specific details/examples to be convincing. | 5 4 3 2 1 0 |
| *Structure* | |
| *Introductory paragraph:* | |
| Has an appropriate opening statement. | 5 4 3 2 1 0 |
| Contains a thesis statement that: | |
| Names items you are comparing. | 5 4 3 2 1 0 |
| States your choice clearly. | 5 4 3 2 1 0 |
| Contains a preview stating relevant criteria for comparison. | 5 4 3 2 1 0 |
| Preview is written as a separate sentence. | 5 4 3 2 1 0 |
| *Paragraphs in body of the message:* | |
| Follow the order established in the preview. | 5 4 3 2 1 0 |
| Begin with a topic sentence. | 5 4 3 2 1 0 |
| Contain topic sentences that develop points given in preview. | 5 4 3 2 1 0 |
| Follow either Diagram 1 or Diagram 2. | 5 4 3 2 1 0 |
| Contain ideas that relate to topic sentence (unity). | 5 4 3 2 1 0 |
| *Concluding paragraph:* | |
| Is four or five sentences long? | 5 4 3 2 1 0 |
| Restates (not copies) the thesis and preview ideas. | 5 4 3 2 1 0 |

*Readability*

| | |
|---|---|
| Transitions appear where necessary between ideas. | 5 4 3 2 1 0 |
| Headings: | |
| Are appropriately formatted. | 5 4 3 2 1 0 |
| Follow the ideas of the preview. | 5 4 3 2 1 0 |
| Grammar | 5 4 3 2 1 0 |
| Word choice | 5 4 3 2 1 0 |
| Punctuation | 5 4 3 2 1 0 |
| Spelling | 5 4 3 2 1 0 |

## EXERCISES

1. Provide a possible purpose for comparing each pair of objects, places, ideas, or people. Then list at least three criteria you would use to make the comparison.

   Two supervisors you have had at work

   *Purpose of comparison:* ______________________________

   ______________________________

   *Criteria / points of comparison:*

   1. ______________________________
   2. ______________________________
   3. ______________________________

   High school writing classes and college writing classes

   *Purpose of comparison:* ______________________________

   ______________________________

   *Criteria / points of comparison:*

   1. ______________________________
   2. ______________________________
   3. ______________________________

   A city vs. a suburb

   *Purpose of comparison:* ______________________________

   ______________________________

   *Criteria / points of comparison:*

   1. ______________________________
   2. ______________________________
   3. ______________________________

*Note:* For exercises 2–9, use separate sheets of paper.

2. For the following pairs, state a purpose for comparison, establish criteria for the comparison, and provide specific supports for each criterion. Use one of the patterns of organization diagrams to organize each comparison/contrast message, and then write the complete message.

   Jesse Jackson and Martin Luther King

   Deregulation of the trucking and airline industries

   Income taxes and property taxes

   Athletics in private colleges and public universities

   Your hometown and another city

   Vegetarians and meat eaters

   Two kinds of karate

   Drug addiction and alcohol abuse

   Two ads for a similar product

   Two professors

   Hard rock and soft rock

3. Compare and contrast the writing classes you had in high school with your writing class or classes now. Remember to establish two or three criteria for comparison before writing.

4. Compare the cost of opening a checking account at two local banks. Use these criteria: minimum balance required, fee for opening the account, cost of checks. Now *recommend* a bank to a friend who is opening a checking account. Include the bank's costs in your description. Your topic sentences should correspond to the criteria, and the criteria themselves can reflect your choice.

5. Compare living at home to living in a dormitory or apartment as a young adult. Decide whether your comparison will include an opinion about the better living arrangement.

6. Compare your ability to cook with the ability of a friend. In your thesis statement, state the purpose of the comparison. Consider comparing cooking ability in relation to preparing a specific dish.

7. Compare the movie version of a book to the book itself or perhaps a movie version of an actual event to the event itself.
8. Compare the discipline of quitting smoking to the discipline of losing weight.
9. Compare this year's clothing fashions to last year's fashions.

## CASES

1. You must buy a dictionary to replace the outdated dictionary you have been using. Because you are able to bring it to your writing class for spelling help, you have decided to purchase a paperback edition rather than a large hardcover edition. Several choices are available in your bookstore. Establish three criteria, or bases for comparison, that correspond to your needs. What do you need most? What features are most important to you? Number of entries? An etymology (gives roots of words)? After listing criteria, compare the contents of the dictionaries and write a paper supporting your choice.
2. You are in charge of arranging a banquet for the Marketing Club's annual awards night at the end of the semester. Two nearby restaurants offer banquet facilities for roughly the same cost. Both offer similar seating capacities and serving arrangements. You decide to choose a restaurant on the basis of the menu. What criteria will you establish to compare menus? After listing at least two criteria, obtain or imagine two menus from the restaurants, compare the menu offerings, and make your recommendation to the Marketing Club. Be sure to mention that the restaurants have comparable facilities and service.
3. You are considering a job transfer that would require you to live overseas. Nations from which you could select include Mexico, Germany, and Japan. Choose one and investigate two or three major cultural differences between your host nation and your home culture. You might choose from the following general list of cultural traits: concepts of time, meeting behaviors, greetings, personal space, nonverbal communication behavior. Write a memo report to your supervisor. State the country you wish to be transferred to. Use the cultural traits as criteria to organize your comparison.
4. Study the two resumes that appear on the following pages. List three criteria you might use to compare the two for the purpose of selecting one person for a part-time retail sales job in a sporting goods store. Then write a rec-

ommendation to the department manager showing that one applicant is better qualified for the position than the other. Base your recommendation on the criteria you established earlier. Use examples from each resume in your specific supports.

# RONALD L. TAFT

**Current address:**
2301 Concord Place (Apt. 4D)
Lawnwood, IL 60601
(312) 787-1000

**Permanent address:**
5681 South Redway Street
Chicago, IL 60621
(312) 284-7780

**CAREER OBJECTIVE:** Creative advertising or sales position in an established advertising firm

## EDUCATION FOR ADVERTISING

Bachelor of Business Administration
Southwestern College, Alton, IL
(Graduation expected: December 1997)

**MAJOR:** Advertising Marketing

**Minors:** Business Communications, Journalism

COURSES IN ADVERTISING

Introduction to Advertising
Retail Advertising
Copywriting

RELATED ELECTIVE COURSES

Public Speaking
Business Communications
Layout and Design

## Activities and Honors

President, Advertising Club
Dean's List, four semesters
Recipient, Academic Scholarship
Boys and Girls Club Volunteer

## Work Experience

Advertising Account Executive, *Southwestern College Herald.* Responsibilities included servicing 20 existing accounts, created six new accounts. (1994–present)

Salesperson, Jeans Warehouse, Chicago, IL. Responsibilities included serving customers, entering sales and returns on cash register. (1992–1994)

Assistant Manager, Bag Room, South Shore Country Club, Chicago, IL. Responsibilities included maintenance of driving range, care of golf carts, equipment rentals. (1991–1992)

Credentials and references upon request

# Scott Forester

6300 N. Russell Street
Chicago, IL 60626
(312) 288-1532

**Objective** To obtain an entry-level position in a manufacturing firm in the Chicago area, in which I can use my education in business

**Education** Bachelor of Business Administration
Southwestern College, Alton, IL
(Degree expected: April 1997)

Associate of Arts, Truman College, Chicago, IL
(Graduated May 1995)

<u>Related Courses</u>

| | |
|---|---|
| Survey of Marketing | Business Finance |
| Principles of Retailing | Financial Accounting |
| Interpersonal Comm. | Business Writing |

Worked since high school to finance college and purchase an automobile.

**Experience** Avondale's Cable TV Marketing, Alton, IL
Salesperson
Duties: selling subscriptions to cable TV
1996–present service; coordinating cable installation

1995 Granny's Shoe Emporium, Evanston, IL
Salesperson, Stocker
Duties: Selling shoes, window displays, and stock room inventory

1994–1993 Collection Agent, *Suburban News,* Skokie, IL
Duties: Examining and auditing accounts.
Phoning and informing newspaper customers of billing status.

1992 Deli Counter Clerk, Jewel Foods, Chicago, IL

**Personal Data** Enjoy baseball, basketball, golf; collect sports cards

# 8 Write Persuasively

*Whether selling your "preowned" car or requesting a grade change, your ability to persuade an audience involves the same critical thinking skills.*

Persuading an audience to accept your point of view means that you must understand how your audience will react to your subject. Will your reader see your subject the same way you do? Or will you need to convince an unbelieving or skeptical audience that your point of view is correct? This chapter begins with a discussion of audience analysis, the critical prewriting process you must complete before developing a key argument. Persuasive appeals involve a broad range of complex issues, such as the psychology of motivation. However, this chapter focuses on the construction of fact-based messages rather than the emotion-based messages of much of the advertising that we are familiar with.

### Audience Analysis

The first step in writing any persuasive message, as with all written messages, is to analyze your audience very carefully. This is extremely important in persuasive writing, for convincing a person to adopt your point of view is a challenge. Your message must appeal to the reader's sense of logic. It must also consider reader attitudes and contain reader benefits. It must also respond to any arguments readers might develop as they read your message. In other words, you must anticipate the questions or counterarguments of your audience.

Analyze the audience for your persuasive message by asking and then answering these questions:

- Whom must I persuade to believe what I have to say?
- What does my audience probably know about this topic?
- What resistance to my point of view can I expect?
- What important information does my audience lack?

You must target a specific audience for your persuasive writing before generating any ideas or supporting information for the argument. For example, persuading an instructor to write a letter of recommendation for a summer job means that you must analyze the instructor, the instructor's response to your request, and the instructor's need for information to put in your letter. Suppose you are going to write to an instructor requesting such a letter. Answer the following questions:

*Whom must I persuade to believe what I have to say?* An instructor of business communication who is currently on vacation and away from the office. I earned a good grade last semester, so the instructor probably has a positive impression of my work.

*What does my audience probably know about this topic?* The instructor knows nothing about the summer job itself, but she knows me and knows the best way to write a recommendation.

*What resistance to my point of view can I expect?* The instructor will have to be persuaded to take time from her vacation schedule to write the letter. I must make the letter writing task as convenient as possible. Enclosing a stamped envelope for the employer to whom she is writing, for example, would make a reply easier.

*What important information does my audience lack?* My instructor will need to know about the position I am applying for, the personal traits she can best address in her letter, and information about dates and the audience for her letter.

Developing an audience profile is the first step in writing a persuasive message. Once you have gathered as much information as you can about the targeted audience, you will be ready to develop the main appeal, or key argument.

## Developing a Key Argument

The best argument to use in your persuasive message will vary according to your audience analysis. Limiting yourself to one major argument has advantages. You can focus your argument and provide more specific, detailed support for your opinion. You can also control the argument by not complicating the issue. Research shows that people are more easily persuaded to vote for a politician if the campaign is focused on a single issue. Keep distracting arguments, or information that doesn't relate specifically to your main argument, out of your persuasive message. You may, of course, cite different reasons or specific information that supports your thesis statement, but the thesis statement itself should address only a central or key argument.

Here are some examples of key arguments based on audience analysis:

*Writing task:* Develop a persuasive message that convinces your instructor to postpone the due date of a major research paper.

*Audience:* A chemistry instructor who has talked a great deal about the importance of deadlines in "the real world" and is usually not receptive to student requests for extra lab time for other minor assignments. However, you know that this instructor also believes that performing a job well is more important than meeting a deadline because he delayed handing out the assignment for the research paper until a typing error was corrected.

*Key argument:* Emphasize the improved quality of work possible with a one-day extension of the due date. Supporting information should appeal to the instructor's belief in quality work (*not* an approach that suggests "if you can be late, why can't we?").

*Thesis statement:* A one-day extension of the deadline for submitting our research could improve the quality of the research papers.

*Writing task:* Prepare a request to your employer for a specific vacation week.

*Audience:* Supervisor who is generally agreeable to employee requests and tries to accommodate everyone's plans for vacations. She is concerned about the upcoming summer season, though, because several key people will be gone at the same time. She may have to consider seniority and project priorities.

*Key argument:* Request your summer vacation date showing her that you will have your project nearly completed. Give her a precisely drawn calendar of your activities before and after the vacation period, including progress on the project.

*Thesis statement* (provide one here): ____________________

______________________________________________________

______________________________________________________

**Organizing Support**

Organizing your support of the thesis statement in a logical pattern can also be persuasive. Develop and organize support for your key argument by considering, once again, the audience analysis. Recall the questions:

- What information does my audience need?
- What information does my audience already have?
- What resistance to my message can I expect?

When you have answered these questions, you have anticipated questions your reader will have as well as information you will need to supply. Outline specific, factual support for your argument that answers likely questions and addresses the concerns your audience might have. Sources of support include facts and figures, statements by authorities, and descriptive examples. Using the two previous key arguments and thesis statements, provide the data to make strong supports in list format.

When you have prepared a simple three- to five-item list of factual supporting data for each of the thesis statements, choose an inductive or deductive pattern to organize the list. Support precedes the key argument in the indirect, inductive pattern. Persuasive messages to resistant audiences are often written inductively so that the support becomes increasingly stronger and ends with the key argument.

Most practical messages appear in direct, deductive pattern, however. If you can assume that your audience is either neutral or positive about your subject, you may present your key argument and then provide specific support. Most audiences prefer the direct method because reading the main idea of a message first saves them time.

If possible, use known audience preferences in ordering your information. For example, in the request to an instructor for a letter of recommendation, the writer should state the request and provide the information in order of importance to the reader. Order of importance in this case might be:

1. A statement about the instructor's vacation and the gratitude the student will feel for the instructor's effort.
2. The name and nature of the position the student is applying for.
3. The qualifications that the student wishes mentioned.
4. The name and address of the employer and the deadline.

Because the student is aware of the imposition created, special acknowledgment of the instructor's generosity with time must be included to be persuasive.

The direct, deductive pattern also provides a logical means of ordering support. The reader will ask why about the thesis statement and then read "because reason 1, reason 2," and so on. Here is a recommendation memo organized according to the direct, deductive method.

> July 7, 19XX
>
> TO: Jay Simpson
>
> FROM: Kay Folmer
>
> SUBJECT: Recommendation to Purchase Avant Copier
>
> We tested both Avant II and Epping copiers over the past leasing period. Our results show that Avant should be our choice for purchase because it meets our criteria of quality, cost, and service. The Avant required 40 percent fewer service calls over the six-month lease period. Avant service representatives appeared within 24 hours of all service requests. Copy quality is comparable for both. However, the Avant is equipped to accept tricolor cartridges should we want to add that option. Finally, the Avant purchase price is $500 less than Epping's cost. We may apply half our rental fees to the purchase.

In this paragraph, the writer takes a direct approach to persuading a neutral audience to accept her recommendation. The key argument is that Avant satisfies the criteria for an office copier: It is efficient and effective. The audience for this message will easily understand the supporting sentences. They appear in the order of the criteria named in the topic sentence and are not unnecessarily repeated in the closing sentence. She has presented facts as support for her conclusion (deductive logic). She has directed her supporting arguments at her supervisor's need to make an economical choice without sacrificing quality and has been brief and specific in giving her proof.

## Summary

Writing persuasively demands close analysis of the audience who receives your message. Who are the readers of this message? What do they know? What will they resist knowing, and how can I overcome this resistance? After a thorough audience analysis, you must then develop your key argument as the theme of your message, develop a variety of support for this theme, and organize the support effectively to persuade your audience to think or do what you ask.

In summary, a persuasive message should be written after careful audience analysis, through evaluation of available information, and logical movement between key arguments and supporting reasons. The exercises that follow are designed for you to practice thinking deductively and organizing a message persuasively. Use clear, concrete language based on rational and objective thinking.

## PERSUASION SCORE SHEET

5=Excellent 4=Good 3=Average 2=Weak 1=Poor 0=Failure

| | |
|---|---|
| *Content* | |
| Opening statement attracts reader's attention. | 5 4 3 2 1 0 |
| Thesis statement gives key argument. | 5 4 3 2 1 0 |
| Factual data is used as support. | 5 4 3 2 1 0 |
| Supporting data is explained convincingly. | 5 4 3 2 1 0 |
| *Structure* | |
| *Introductory paragraph:* | |
| Has an appropriate opening statement. | 5 4 3 2 1 0 |
| Contains thesis statement that states position clearly. | 5 4 3 2 1 0 |
| Contains a preview that: | |
| States main supporting ideas. | 5 4 3 2 1 0 |
| Is written as a separate sentence. | 5 4 3 2 1 0 |
| *Paragraphs in body of the message:* | |
| Follow the order established in the preview. | 5 4 3 2 1 0 |
| Begin with a topic sentence. | 5 4 3 2 1 0 |
| Contain topic sentences that: | |
| Develop points given in preview. | 5 4 3 2 1 0 |
| Support the thesis. | 5 4 3 2 1 0 |
| Contain data that relates to topic sentence (unity). | 5 4 3 2 1 0 |
| *Concluding paragraph:* | |
| Is four or five sentences long. | 5 4 3 2 1 0 |
| Restates (not copies) the thesis and preview ideas. | 5 4 3 2 1 0 |

*Readability*

| | |
|---|---|
| Transitions appear where necessary between ideas. | 5 4 3 2 1 0 |
| Headings: | |
| Are appropriately formatted. | 5 4 3 2 1 0 |
| Follow ideas of preview. | 5 4 3 2 1 0 |
| Grammar | 5 4 3 2 1 0 |
| Word choice | 5 4 3 2 1 0 |
| Punctuation | 5 4 3 2 1 0 |
| Spelling | 5 4 3 2 1 0 |

## EXERCISES

1. After reading each description of the writing task, identify the audience of the written message, key argument that you would develop, and supporting reasons for the key argument.

   *Task A:* You have discovered an error in the point total you have accumulated for a college course. You intend to write a message to the instructor requesting a grade change.

   *Audience:* ______________________________

   *Key argument:* ______________________________

   ______________________________

   *Supporting reasons for argument:* ______________________________

   ______________________________

   ______________________________

   ______________________________

   ______________________________

   ______________________________

   ______________________________

   ______________________________

   *Task B:* You would like a refund for the money you spent on a faulty product. (You provide the name of the product.)

   *Audience:* ______________________________

   *Key Argument:* ______________________________

   ______________________________

   *Supporting reasons for argument:* ______________________________

   ______________________________

   ______________________________

   ______________________________

   ______________________________

   ______________________________

   ______________________________

   ______________________________

*Task C:* You must write a cover letter to a prospective employer to accompany your resume.

*Audience:* ______________________________

*Key argument:* ______________________________

______________________________

*Supporting reasons for argument:* ______________________________

______________________________

______________________________

______________________________

______________________________

______________________________

______________________________

______________________________

*Task D:* You are recommending a particular professional (lawyer, accountant, doctor, barber, dry cleaner).

*Audience:* ______________________________

*Key argument:* ______________________________

______________________________

*Supporting reasons for argument:* ______________________________

______________________________

______________________________

______________________________

______________________________

______________________________

______________________________

______________________________

*Task E:* You are recommending a restaurant for a wedding reception.

*Audience:* ______________________________

*Key Argument:* ______________________________

______________________________

*Supporting reasons for argument:* ______________________________

______________________________

______________________________

______________________________

______________________________

______________________________

______________________________

______________________________

*Task F:* You have to write a report recommending a stock to buy for an individual investor.

*Audience:* ______________________________

*Key argument:* ______________________________

______________________________

*Supporting reasons for argument:* ______________________________

______________________________

______________________________

______________________________

______________________________

______________________________

______________________________

______________________________

2. For each of the tasks outlined in the preceding exercise, compose a topic sentence addressed to the main audience.

   *Task A topic sentence:* ______________________________

   ______________________________________________

   ______________________________________________

   *Task B topic sentence:* ______________________________

   ______________________________________________

   ______________________________________________

   *Task C topic sentence:* ______________________________

   ______________________________________________

   ______________________________________________

   *Task D topic sentence:* ______________________________

   ______________________________________________

   ______________________________________________

   *Task E topic sentence:* ______________________________

   ______________________________________________

   ______________________________________________

   *Task F topic sentence:* ______________________________

   ______________________________________________

   ______________________________________________

3. Write a complete paragraph for one of the tasks in the preceding exercise. Begin with the topic sentence containing the key argument and provide rational support in logically ordered sentences. You may create facts and examples for use in the supporting sentences.

## CASES

1. Persuade a specific, neutral audience to share your point of view on one of the following subjects after first narrowing the key argument for use as a thesis statement. Use facts, not opinions, for support. Write a message in report format, including an introductory paragraph and supporting paragraphs. For example:

   *Subject:* Financial aid to college students

   *Narrowed key argument for thesis statement:* College students claimed as dependents by parents should be eligible for student loans regardless of parents' income.

   *Subjects*

   Bilingual education

   On-site preschools at corporations

   State-sponsored lotteries

   Supporting the fine arts (e.g., symphony orchestras, museums) with tax money

   Physical exercise

   Organized sports for children

   A healthy diet

   Sports stars as role models

   Compulsory national service

   On-the-job drug testing

   Budgeting

*Subject:* ______________________________

*Key argument:* ______________________________

______________________________

*Report:* ______________________________

2. Alpha Corporation has five salespeople who cover a 500-square-mile territory. They spend four of five workdays a week traveling and visiting customers. During that time, communication between office personnel and salespeople is difficult. Also, the salespeople have a hard time accessing product information to answer customers' questions when they are on the road.

   You have just learned of a new communications tool that might help to solve these problems. It is a small computer called a PDA (personal digital assistant). Several computer companies make PDAs. You collect brochures from several computer stores in your area. You are so impressed with the features they describe that you decide to write a memo to your supervisor, Alpha's director of marketing, proposing a pilot program to test a PDA in use. Use the features of the PDA you choose to write about to support your key argument.

Date: ______________________

To: ______________________

From: ______________________

Subject: ______________________

3. As a member of various organizations, you have probably noticed areas that need improvement. List all the formal groups that you belong to. (Consider your work, professional, civic, and social organizations.) For each group, name as many problem areas as you can think of. (Your group may not have a "problem," but almost every group has an area that could be improved by a change in procedure.) Study the areas that you have listed. Pick one to develop as the subject of a persuasive memo written to the head of the organization.

Date: ____________________

To: ____________________

From: ____________________

Subject: ____________________

# A Letter and Memo Formats

*Format* refers to placement of the parts of a message on a page. The two most common short business formats are letters and memos. Every organization may pick a formatting style and tailor it to its own needs and tastes. In this appendix you will learn two styles of letters and memos out of several styles that exist. Use these styles when responding to problems in this textbook unless you are otherwise instructed.

## Letters

One chooses a letter format primarily for external communication, that is, for communication with someone *outside* the organization. For example, if you worked for the ABC Corporation and were communicating in writing with someone at Omega, Inc., you would use letter format for your message. Letters have seven standard parts:

1. *Heading:* Either the letterhead printed on company stationery (see model 1) or the writer's address (see model 2). The state name should be abbreviated, using the two-

letter postal service abbreviation. The zip code should always be included.

2. *Date:* The month, day, and year that the letter is written.
3. *Inside address:* The full name, courtesy title (Mr. or Ms.), or professional title (Dr., Rev., Col., etc.) of the person you are writing, his/her job title (Director, Assistant Manager, Vice President, etc.), the department he/she works in, organization name, street, city, state, and zip code of the person you are writing to.
4. *Salutation:* "Dear" is the standard business salutation.

   *Example:* Dear Ms. Fisher: Dear Dr. Phelps:
   Dear Ralph:

   [Notice that a colon (:) follows the name in the salutation.]
5. *Body:* Single-space paragraphs of the body of a letter; insert double spaces between paragraphs.
6. *Complimentary close:* "Sincerely" and "Cordially" are standard closes in business.
7. *Signature block:* Sign your letter above your typed signature

Letters also have a few additional parts, such as enclosure notations, copy notations, and second page headings.

8. *Enclosure notation:* When you send something with a letter, such as a form, map, check, picture, etc., type the word "Enclosure" after your typewritten signature. (Use the plural, "Enclosures," if you are sending more than one item.)
9. *Copy notation:* When you are sending a copy of the letter to a person in addition to the person to whom you addressed the letter, you type the word "Copy" after the Enclosure notation. (Use the plural, "Copies," if you are sending copies to two or more people.)
10. *Second-page heading:* When your letter extends to two or more pages, use a heading on the second and succeeding pages. This heading lists the name of the person to whom you are writing, the date of the letter, and the page number.

    *Example:* Ms. Emily Stark, June 6, 1996, p. 2

## MODEL 1: LETTER FOR COMPANY BUSINESS

If you are writing *as your company's representative* to another company, you would use your company's letterhead stationery. The printed letterhead is a *heading* that includes the name, address, and telephone number of your company. It may also include other information such as telex, fax number, e-mail address, company logo, etc. The printed letterhead may be in the middle of the page or on either margin, depending on the design the organization has adopted.

| | |
|---|---|
| *Heading* | The ABC Corporation<br>4700 Industrial Drive<br>York, PA 17407-4841 |
| | (717) 555-1212 |
| • | |
| • | |
| *Date* | June 6, 1996 |
| • | |
| • | |
| *Inside address* | Ms. Emily Stark, Director<br>Human Resources Department<br>Omega, Inc.<br>77 West Palatine Drive<br>Milton, PA 17702 |
| ◊ | |
| *Salutation* | Dear Ms. Stark: |
| ◊ | |
| *Body* | Brian Etters, a systems analyst at your company, has listed you as a reference on his application for employment with us. |
| ◊ | |
| | We would very much appreciate your describing Mr. Etters' skills and work habits on the enclosed form. |
| ◊ | |
| *Complimentary close* | Sincerely, |
| ◊ | |
| ◊ | |
| ◊ | |
| *Typewritten name / title* | Veronica Dunn, Manager |
| *Department name* | Information Systems |
| • | |
| • | |
| | Enclosure |
| | Copy: A. H. Lieber, Personnel |

• *variable spacing*
◊ *one blank space*

If you are writing a letter for *personal* business, that is, your own business, rather than business you are conducting as company representative, use your own address rather than a company letterhead as the heading of your letter. Some people, of course, have their own personal letterhead stationery. However, if you are typing your letter on a blank sheet of paper, it should look like this:

| | |
|---|---|
| *Heading* | 120 Gloria Drive<br>Jacobus, PA 17407 |
| *Date* | June 17, 1996 |
| • | |
| • | |
| *Inside address* | Ms. Veronica Dunn, Manager<br>Information Systems<br>The ABC Corporation<br>4700 Industrial Drive<br>York, PA 17407-4841 |
| ◊ | |
| *Salutation* | Dear Ms. Stark: |
| ◊ | |
| *Body* | Thank you very much for spending time with me Monday morning and for giving me a tour of your facilities. |
| ◊ | |
| | I was very pleased to learn that my course work in computer science at Southeastern prepared me so well for a position such as you are offering. |
| ◊ | |
| | If you would like further information about my educational background or work experience, please call me at (717) 248-0998. |
| ◊ | |
| *Complimentary close* | Sincerely, |
| ◊ | |
| ◊ | |
| ◊ | |
| *Typewritten name* | Brian Etters |

• *variable spacing*
◊ *one blank space*

## Memos

You use memo format for internal communication, that is, for communication with someone *inside* your organization. For example, if you are in human resources and need to send a written message to someone in marketing, you would use memo format.

Memos have four standard headings:

1. *Date:* The month, day, and year that the memo was written.
2. *To:* The name of the recipient of the memo.
3. *From:* The writer's name.
4. *Subject:* The topic of the memo.

These headings are typically followed by a colon (:). The paragraphs of memos are single-spaced with double spaces between paragraphs.

Additional parts of memos are attachment notations, copy notations, and second page headings.

5. *Attachment notations* serve the same purpose as enclosure notations in letters. The name is different because items are literally attached to a memo with staples or paper clips, whereas items are enclosed, in an envelope, with a letter.
6. *Copy notations* and *second-page headings* follow the same form and have the same function in memos as in letters.

DATE: June 1, 1996

◊

TO: Emily Stark, Director
Human Resources Department

◊

FROM: Brian Etters, Intern
Computer Information Systems

◊

SUBJECT: Request for Reference

◊

May I list you as a reference for jobs I am currently applying for?

◊

As you know, when I finish my internship with Omega, I will be looking for a full-time position in computer systems in southeastern Pennsylvania. I already have a few leads on openings in that area. Your recommendation will be most helpful in my obtaining a position.

◊

Please let me know whether you will be willing to speak to prospective employers or write letters of recommendation on my behalf. You can reach me at x76.

• *variable spacing*
◊ *one blank space*

# B Proposals and Progress Reports

Proposals and progress reports are two common business documents. Proposals help organizations get new business and initiate policy changes. Progress reports keep supervisors and customers up to date on the status of major projects.

## Proposals

Proposals are persuasive documents that advocate change. They may favor change in the way something is done, offer to solve problems, or introduce new ideas. They may be as short as a two-page memo or as long as a book. They may be internal; that is, employees may suggest ways that companies or other organizations to which they belong may change, or students may write to convince an instructor that they can undertake an academic project. They may be external, that is, coming from a potential client outside the organization. They may be solicited, that is, written in response to a request for proposal, or unsolicited. Whatever the dimensions or purpose of the proposal, all proposals have several common elements. These are explained in the following plan for a proposal.

*Introduction*

In the introduction, cover these concerns:

- *The problem:* Explain the problem briefly, summarizing why the change you propose should be undertaken.
- *The purpose:* Explain the purpose of the proposal.
- *The benefits:* Explain the benefits of successfully completing the project that is being proposed.

Close the introduction with an overview of topics presented in the body of the proposal.

*Body*

In the body of the proposal, describe in detail what you plan to do and how you plan to do it.

- *Old system:* Describe what is wrong with the old system to show that the need for change exists.
- *New system:* Describe what *should* happen, explaining step by step how to make it happen and detailing the advantages of the new system.

  Provide complete information to persuade the reader to accept the proposal.

  Make sure that information is internally consistent, that one part of the proposal does not contradict another part.

  Check that what you propose is workable.
- *Work plan:* Give a calendar of dates (in list form) to show when you plan to accomplish each *specific* step in the project.
- *Personnel:* Describe the knowledge and experience that will enable you and possible collaborators to complete the project. (Mention similar tasks that you have successfully completed, if possible.)
- *Facilities and equipment:* Describe everything you need to complete the project (for example, space, secretarial help, equipment, supplies).
- *Budget:* Identify your expenditures in monetary terms. Sometimes a form for the budget is given and the writer has only to fill in appropriate blanks. If no form is given, list and total the expenditures.

*Conclusion*

In the conclusion of the proposal, summarize the main points you have covered to reinforce them in the reader's mind.

- Reemphasize need for the project.
- Describe present and future benefits from completion of the project.

## Progress Reports

People who work on long-term projects often must report their progress to their supervisors one or more times between the starting date of the project and its completion. These progress reports are generally short documents, often in memo format. Their purpose is to let the supervisor know the status of a project: Is it on track? What kind of information is the writer finding? Is the writer encountering obstacles or setbacks that will delay completion of the project? A simple progress report may be organized chronologically, using headings like "Completed Work" and "Remaining Work."

- Name the project you are working on.

*Completed Work*

- Explain what you have accomplished to date. Relate accomplishments to the original schedule and the goals of the project.
- Name any obstacles or setbacks you have encountered. Describe how you plan to overcome them.

*Remaining Work*

- Submit a schedule reflecting changes that you have had to make.
- Describe the work that remains and how you expect to accomplish it.
- Conclude by assuring your supervisor that the project will be done on time or asking for a time extension (or assistance) if necessary.

# C Documenting Secondary Sources

In both academic and professional writing, you will sometimes need to document secondary sources. *To document* a secondary source is to identify from whom and where you got information. Typical secondary sources are books; magazine, newspaper or journal articles; and encyclopedias and other reference works. Other secondary sources may be pamphlets, letters, and interviews.

## Reasons for Documentation

Any time you use someone else's words in a direct quotation or their ideas in a paraphrase or summary, you must give that person credit in a note called a *citation.* Citations appear both in the text of the paper or report that you are writing and in a list, called a bibliography or "Works Cited" list, at the end of your report.

The reasons for giving credit through citation of sources are as follows:

1. You are showing your readers that you have done your "homework." You have been thorough in finding and presenting the latest, most up-to-date information on your subject.
2. You have proved or backed up your ideas with additional information from other authors. You have also informed your readers about how they can find more information if they wish to do further research themselves.
3. You have followed ethical and legal guidelines by giving appropriate credit to original authors for their words and ideas.

## Keys to Documentation

Two keys to documentation are following a consistent format for citations and giving full, accurate information in citations.

Two guides to ensure formatting consistency in your documentation are those recommended by the Modern Language Association of America (MLA) in the *MLA Handbook for Writers of Research Papers* and the American Psychological Association (APA) in the *Publication Manual of the American Psychological Association.* Other guides are available, and you should use whatever is recommended by your instructor or supervisor. In this textbook, you will be following MLA format for citations.

The kinds of citations you will be studying here are *parenthetical* citations, which occur in the text that you are writing, and citations on the "Works Cited" list at the end of your paper or report. Parenthetical citations are shortened citations that appear in parentheses; hence their name. The full information for each parenthetical citation appears in the "Works Cited" list.

### Parenthetical Citations

When you are documenting the words or ideas of another writer, you give that writer credit for the words or ideas in the text. Specifically, you write the author's name and the number of the page the information is found on and put this information in parentheses. The following is an example of parenthetical citation:

> Although IBM has lagged in the development of new computer technology, customers remain loyal because of the quality of service the company delivers (Peters and Waterman 157).

Notice the following:

1. This example is not in quotation marks; thus, we know it's a paraphrase of the original authors' (Peters and Waterman's) words.
2. The parenthesis comes *before* the period that ends the sentence.
3. No punctuation separates the authors' names from the number of the page on which the information is found, nor does the word or abbreviation for the word *page* appear.

A second method for giving this information and citing it in the text of your report follows:

> Peters and Waterman note that, while IBM has developed little new computer technology, the company has kept its customers by serving them well (157).

In this form of citation, the authors' names appear in the text, and only the page number is in parentheses. This method is also acceptable in MLA format.

The author-page number format is useful in most instances. One other format you should be aware of to achieve full clarity is the author-title-page number format. This format is useful when you have two or more works by the same author or authors. For example, Joyce Lain Kennedy and Thomas J. Morrow have coauthored two books. If you were using information from both books in your report, you would have to add the titles in your parenthetical citations to distinguish between them. The following examples show you how to write this kind of citation:

> The place to find a job these days is in small business. But small businesses are contracting with resume database services as a way to keep costs down and to find current candidates (Kennedy and Morrow, *Electronic Resume Revolution* 14). One such database service, Electronic Job Matching, keeps on-line resumes active for four months or until the job

candidate has obtained employment (Kennedy and Morrow, *Electronic Job Search Revolution* 47).

**Works Cited List**

The "Works Cited" list at the end of the report gives the full citation for all books, articles, or other works you cited parenthetically in the text of your report. A few rules apply to the format of this list:

1. The heading "Works Cited" appears centered on the first page of your list.
2. Citations appear in alphabetical order:

   By authors' last names.

   By the name of the corporation or organization that produced the book if no author is listed.

   By the first significant word of the title of the work (*A, An,* and *The* are not significant words) if no author is listed.
3. Citations are double-spaced.
4. The second and all subsequent lines of citations are indented five spaces.

The following guide introduces you to some common citation formats. If you need more information, check your library or bookstore for a copy of the *MLA Handbook for Writers of Research Papers,* 4th ed. (New York: MLA, 1995) by Joseph Gibaldi.

*Book with One Author*

Krol, Ed. *The Whole Internet: User's Guide and Catalog.* Sebastopol, CA: O'Reilly, 1992.

*Book with Two Authors*

Pascarelli, Emil F., and Deborah Quilter. *Repetitive Strain Injury: A Computer User's Guide.* New York: John Wiley, 1994.

*Book with Three Editors*

Bruce, Bertram, Joy Kreeft Peyton, and Trent Batson, eds. *Network-Based Classrooms: Promises and Realities.* New York: Cambridge UP, 1993.

["UP" stands for University Press, the recommended abbreviation for citations.]

*Book with Corporate Authorship*

Corporation for Public Broadcasting. *Evaluating Student Outcomes from Telecourse Instruction.* Santa Monica: Rand, 1986.

*Journal Article*

Carbone, Mary T. "The History and Development of Business Communication Principles: 1776–1916." *The Journal of Business Communication* 31 (1994): 173–93.

*Magazine Article*

Richards, Rhonda. "Take Care of Business: Young Entrepreneurs Go for Their Dreams." *Essence,* September, 1994, pp. 66–68, 70.

*Encyclopedia Article*

"Minimum Wage." *The World Book Encyclopedia.* 1993 ed.

*Personal Interview*

Steinem, Gloria. Personal interview. 15 January 1995.

*Published Interview*

Huston, John. Interview. *Reflections in a Male Eye: John Huston and the American Experience.* By John Huston, Gaylyn Studlar, and David Desser. Washington, Smithsonian Institution Press, 1993.

*Telephone Interview*

Clinton, Hillary. Telephone interview. 1 September 1994.

*Newspaper Article*

Jacobson, Robert L. "Computerized Testing Runs Into Trouble." *Chronicle of Higher Education* 3 August 1994:, A16–A17.

# Index


Abstract ideas, description of, 64-65
Attachment notations, memos, 171
Audience analysis, 2-4
  characteristics of, 3-4
  expectations of, 3-4
  ideas useful for, 3
  and persuasive writing, 148-49, 153

Body:
  defined, 89
  letters, 168
  proposals, 174-75
Brainstorming, 1-2, 16-17

Case studies, paragraphs, 40-41
Citations, parenthetical, 178-80
Clear thinking, and good writing, 1
Coherence, 37-39
  and empathy, 38
  paragraphs, 37-39
Comparisons, 131-46
  cases, 143-46
  Comparison/Contrast Score Sheet, 138-39
  criteria, 132-34
  definition of, 131-32
  exercises, 140-42
  methods of development, 134-36
Complimentary close, letters, 168
Concluding paragraph, 91-92
Conclusion, proposals, 175
Contrasts, 131-46
  cases, 143-46
  Comparison/Contrast Score Sheet, 138-39
  definition of, 131
  exercises, 140-42

Copy notations:
  letters, 168
  memos, 171
Corporate authorship, books with, citation
  formats, 181

Date:
  letters, 168
  memos, 171
Decision making, 132
Description, 63-82
  Description Score Sheet, 69
  exercises, 70-82
  outline for, 65-67
  principles of, 64-65
  spatial relationships, 67
Documenting secondary sources, *See* Secondary sources, documenting
Drafts, 1

Empathy, and coherence, 38
Enclosure notation, letters, 168
Encyclopedia articles, citation formats, 181
Essays, 6

Factual information, beginning messages with, 88
Format:
  of letters, defined, 167
  of written messages, 6
Freewriting, 18-20
From: line, memos, 171

Heading, 89
  letters, 167-68, 169
  printed letterhead as, 169
  sample report with, 90-92
Historical background, beginning messages with, 87

Idea generation techniques, 15-20
  brainstorming, 16-17
  exercises, 26-32
  freewriting, 18-20
  mapping, 17-18
Illustrations, in process descriptions, 112-13
Inside address, letters, 168
Introductory paragraph:
  longer messages, 86-88
  message preview, 88
  proposals, 174

Journal articles, citation formats, 181

Lab report, writing, 113-15
Letters, 6, 167-70
  body, 168
  complimentary close, 168
  copy notation, 168
  date, 168
  enclosure notation, 168
  heading, 167-68, 169
  inside address, 168
  for personal business, 170
  printed letterhead, 169
  salutation, 168
  second-page heading, 168
  signature block, 168
Longer messages, 83-107
  body of message, 89
  cases, 101-7
  concluding paragraph, 91-92
  exercises, 94-100
  headings, 89
    sample report with, 90-91
  introductory paragraph, 86-88
  Longer Message Score Sheet, 93
  message preview, 88
  outline for, 84

Longer messages (*cont.*)
reader aids, 86-89
structure of, 83-86

Magazine articles, citation formats, 181
Mapping, 17-18
Memos, 6, 170
attachment notations, 171
copy notations, 171
paragraphs, 171
second-page headings, 171
Message preview, 88
*MLA Handbook for Writers of Research Papers,* 178, 180

Newspaper articles, citation formats, 181

One-author books, citation formats, 180
Opening statement, introductory paragraph, 86-88
Outline, for description, 65-67
Outlining, 20-24
organizing information by, 20-21
outline logic, using, 23-24
three-step outline, 21-23

Paragraphs, 6, 33-41
business cases, 47-51
Case Analysis and Response Checklist, 42
case studies, 40-41
coherence, 37-39
exercises, 44-46
memos, 171
outline for, 84
Paragraph Score Sheet, 43
putting writing into perspective, 39-40
rules for writing, 33-34
science and technology cases, 52-56
social and sciences and liberal arts cases, 57-61
supporting sentences, 37
topic sentences, 34-36
Parenthetical citations, 178-80
Personal interviews, citation formats, 181
Persuasive writing, 147-65
audience analysis, 148-49, 153
cases, 161-66
exercises, 156-60
key argument, developing, 149-50
organizing support, 150-52
Persuasion Score Sheet, 154-55
Primary audience, 2
Printed letterhead, 169
Problem solving, 132
Process description, 109-30
cases, 124-30
definition of, 109
exercises, 120-23
format for, 116-17
illustrating, 112-13
lab report, writing, 113-15
Process Description Score Sheet, 119
writing, 110-12
Progress reports, 175
Proposals, 173-75
body, 174-75
conclusion, 175
definition of, 173
introduction, 174
*Publication Manual of the American Psychological Association,* 178
Published interviews, citation formats, 181

Question, beginning messages with, 87
Quotation, beginning messages with, 87

Reader-initiated messages, 5
Research papers, 6

Salutation, letters, 168
Secondary audience, 2
Secondary sources, documenting, 177-81
keys to documentation, 178-81
parenthetical citations, 178-80
reasons for documentation, 177-78
Works Cited list, 180-81
Second-page headings:
letters, 168
memos, 171
Signature block, letters, 168
Spatial relationships, 67
Subject: line, memos, 171
Subtopics, 65
Supporting sentences, 37

Telephone interviews, citation formats, 181
Thinking skills, and description, 64
Three-editor books, citation formats, 180-81
Three-step outline, 21-23
To: line, memos, 171
Topic sentences, 34-36, 65
first, main idea of, 89
Two-author books, citation formats, 180

Vertical logic, 24

Works Cited list, 180-81
Writer-initiated messages, 5
Writing:
general purposes of, 5-6
putting into perspective, 39-40
Written messages, format of, 6